SERIES

A life-changing encounter
with God's Word from the books of

COLOSSIANS
& PHILEMON

D1279419

A NavPress resource published in alliance
with Tyndale House Publishers, Inc.

NAVPRESS⬤

NavPress is the publishing ministry of The Navigators, an international Christian organization and leader in personal spiritual development. NavPress is committed to helping people grow spiritually and enjoy lives of meaning and hope through personal and group resources that are biblically rooted, culturally relevant, and highly practical.

For more information, visit www.NavPress.com.

CONTENTS

ACKNOWLEDGMENTS

The LifeChange series has been produced through the coordinated efforts of a team of Navigator Bible study developers and NavPress editorial staff, along with a nationwide network of field-testers.

Series Editor: Karen Lee-Thorp

HOW TO USE THIS STUDY

Objectives

Most guides in the LifeChange series of Bible studies cover one book of the Bible. Although the LifeChange guides vary with the books they explore, they share some common goals:

1. To provide you with a firm foundation of understanding and a thirst to return to the book.
2. To teach you by example how to study a book of the Bible without structured guides.
3. To give you all the historical background, word definitions, and explanatory notes you need so that your only other reference is the Bible.
4. To help you grasp the message of the book as a whole.
5. To teach you how to let God's Word transform you into Christ's image.

Each lesson in this study is designed to take sixty to ninety minutes to complete on your own. The guide is based on the assumption that you are completing one lesson per week, but if time is limited you can do half a lesson per week or whatever amount allows you to be thorough.

Flexibility

LifeChange guides are flexible, allowing you to adjust the quantity and depth of your study to meet your individual needs. The guide offers many optional questions in addition to the regular numbered questions. The optional questions, which appear in the margins of the study pages, include the following:

Optional Application. Nearly all application questions are optional; we hope you will do as many as you can without overcommitting yourself.

For Thought and Discussion. Beginning Bible students should be able to handle these, but even advanced students need to think about them. These questions frequently deal with ethical issues and other biblical principles.

They often offer cross-references to spark thought, but the references do not give obvious answers. They are good for group discussions.

For Further Study. These include: (a) cross-references that shed light on a topic the book discusses, and (b) questions that delve deeper into the passage. You can omit them to shorten a lesson without missing a major point of the passage.

If you are meeting in a group, decide together which optional questions to prepare for each lesson, and how much of the lesson you will cover at the next meeting. Normally, the group leader should make this decision, but you might let each member choose his or her own application questions.

As you grow in your walk with God, you will find the LifeChange guide growing with you—a helpful reference on a topic, a continuing challenge for application, a source of questions for many levels of growth.

Overview and details

The study begins with an overview of Colossians. The key to interpretation is context—what is the whole passage or book *about?*—and the key to context is purpose—what is the author's *aim* for the whole work? In lesson 1 you will lay the foundation for your study of Colossians by asking yourself, *Why did the author (and God) write the book? What did they want to accomplish? What is the book about?*

In lessons 2 through 9, you will analyze successive passages of Colossians in detail. Thinking about how a paragraph fits into the overall goal of the book will help you to see its purpose. Its purpose will help you see its meaning. Frequently reviewing a chart or outline of the book will enable you to make these connections.

In lesson 10, you will review Colossians, returning to the big picture to see whether your view of it has changed after closer study. Review will also strengthen your grasp of major issues and give you an idea of how you have grown from your study.

Lesson 11 covers Philemon, a short letter Paul wrote to a Christian in Colosse.

Kinds of questions

Bible study on your own—without a structured guide—follows a progression. First you observe: What does the passage *say?* Then you interpret: What does the passage *mean?* Lastly you apply: How does this truth *affect* my life?

Some of the "how" and "why" questions will take some creative thinking, even prayer, to answer. Some are opinion questions without clear-cut right answers; these will lend themselves to discussions and side studies.

Don't let your study become an exercise in knowledge alone. Treat the passage as God's Word, and stay in dialogue with Him as you study. Pray, "Lord, what do You want me to see here?" "Father, why is this true?" "Lord, how does this apply to my life?"

6

It is important that you write down your answers. The act of writing clarifies your thinking and helps you to remember.

Study aids

A list of reference materials, including a few notes of explanation to help you make good use of them, begins on page 135. This guide is designed to include enough background to let you interpret with just your Bible and the guide. Still, if you want more information on a subject or want to study a book on your own, try the references listed.

Scripture versions

Unless otherwise indicated, the Bible quotations in this guide are from the New International Version of the Bible. Other versions cited are the Revised Standard Version (RSV), the New American Standard Bible (NASB), the New English Bible (NEB), the New King James Version (NKJV), and the King James Version (KJV).

Use any translation you like for study, preferably more than one. A paraphrase such as The Living Bible is not accurate enough for study, but it can be helpful for comparison or devotional reading.

Memorizing and meditating

A psalmist wrote, "I have hidden your word in my heart that I might not sin against you" (Psalm 119:11). If you write down a verse or passage that challenges or encourages you and reflect on it often for a week or more, you will find it beginning to affect your motives and actions. We forget quickly what we read once; we remember what we ponder.

When you find a significant verse or passage, you might copy it onto a card to keep with you. Set aside five minutes during each day just to think about what the passage might mean in your life. Recite it over to yourself, exploring its meaning. Then, return to your passage as often as you can during your day, for a brief review. You will soon find it coming to mind spontaneously.

For group study

A group of four to ten people allows the richest discussions, but you can adapt this guide for other sized groups. It will suit a wide range of group types, such as home Bible studies, growth groups, youth groups, and businessmen's studies. Both new and experienced Bible students, and new and mature Christians, will benefit from the guide. You can omit or leave for later years any questions you find too easy or too hard.

The guide is intended to lead a group through one lesson per week. However, feel free to split lessons if you want to discuss them more thoroughly. Or, omit some questions in a lesson if preparation or discussion time is limited. You can always return to this guide for personal study later. You will be able to discuss only a few questions at length, so choose some for discussion and others for background. Make time at each discussion for members to ask about anything they didn't understand.

Each lesson in the guide ends with a section called "For the group." These sections give advice on how to focus a discussion, how you might apply the lesson in your group, how you might shorten a lesson, and so on. The group leader should read each "For the group" at least a week ahead so that he or she can tell the group how to prepare for the next lesson.

Each member should prepare for a meeting by writing answers for all of the background and discussion questions to be covered. If the group decides not to take an hour per week for private preparation, then expect to take at least two meetings per lesson to work through the questions. Application will be very difficult, however, without private thought and prayer.

Two reasons for studying in a group are accountability and support. When each member commits in front of the rest to seek growth in an area of life, you can pray with one another, listen jointly for God's guidance, help one another to resist temptation, assure each other that the other's growth matters to you, use the group to practice spiritual principles, and so on. Pray about one another's commitments and needs at most meetings. Spend the first few minutes of each meeting sharing any results from applications prompted by previous lessons. Then discuss new applications toward the end of the meeting. Follow such sharing with prayer for these and other needs.

If you write down each other's applications and prayer requests, you are more likely to remember to pray for them during the week, ask about them at the next meeting, and notice answered prayers. You might want to get a notebook for prayer requests and discussion notes.

Notes taken during discussion will help you to remember, follow up on ideas, stay on the subject, and clarify a total view of an issue. But don't let note-taking keep you from participating. Some groups choose one member at each meeting to take notes. Then someone copies the notes and distributes them at the next meeting. Rotating these tasks can help include people. Some groups have someone take notes on a large pad of paper or erasable marker board so that everyone can see what has been recorded.

Pages 138–139 list some good sources of counsel for leading group studies.

PAUL AND COLOSSE
Historical Background

Map of the Roman Empire

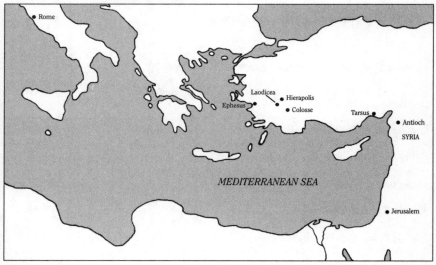

Although Paul wrote to the church at Colosse from house arrest in Rome the power of Christ was not chained. Throughout his refutation of heresy, Paul points out that Christ is the image of God, the sustainer, the source. Even if some new, attractive teaching seems substantial, it is hollow and deceptive next to the fullness of Christ. By demonstrating the supremacy of Christ, Paul hopes to refocus the attention of the Colossians "on things above, where Christ is, seated at the right hand of God" (3:1).

Saul the Pharisee

Some knowledge of Paul's background helps us understand his views on the issues being debated in Colosse. He was born in the first decade AD in

Timeline of Paul's Ministry

(All dates are approximate, based on F. F. Bruce, *Paul: Apostle of the Heart Set Free*, page 475.)

Public ministry of Jesus	AD 28–30
Conversion of Paul (Acts 9:1-19)	33
Paul visits Jerusalem to see Peter (Galatians 1:18)	35
Paul in Cilicia and Syria (Galatians 1:21; Acts 9:30)	35–46
Paul visits Jerusalem to clarify the mission to the Gentiles (Galatians 2:1-10)	46
Paul and Barnabas in Cyprus and Galatia (Acts 13–14)	47–48
Letter to the Galatians	48?
Council of Jerusalem (Acts 15)	49
Paul and Silas travel from Antioch to Asia Minor, Macedonia, and Achaia (Acts 16–17)	49–50
Letters to the Thessalonians	50
Paul in Corinth (Acts 18:1-18)	50–52
Paul visits Jerusalem	52
Paul in Ephesus (Acts 19)	52–55
Letters to the Corinthians	55–56
Paul travels to Macedonia, Dalmatia, and Achaia (Acts 20)	55–57
Letter to the Romans	early 57
Paul to Jerusalem (Acts 21:1–23:22)	May 57
Paul imprisoned in Caesarea (Acts 23:23–26:32)	57–59
Paul sent to house arrest in Rome (Acts 27:1–28:31)	59–62
Letters to Philippians, Colossians, Ephesians, Philemon	60?–62
Letters to Timothy and Titus	?
Paul executed in Rome	65?

Tarsus, a prosperous city on the trade route from Syria to Asia Minor. Tarsus was known for its schools of philosophy and liberal arts, and some scholars believe that Paul must have had some contact with these. Like most cities in the Roman Empire, Tarsus probably contained synagogues of Greek-speaking Jews who were often as devout as their Hebrew-speaking brethren.[1]

However, Paul called himself "a Hebrew of Hebrews" (Philippians 3:5), which probably means that his parents spoke Hebrew and raised him in a strict Jewish home, isolated as much as possible from the pagan city around them.[2] They named their boy "Saul" after Israel's first king, the most glorious member of the tribe of Benjamin, to which Saul's parents traced their ancestry (see Philippians 3:5). It was a rare Jew outside Palestine who could trace a pure lineage back to the ancient days of Israel, and fellow Jews would have envied the pedigree. Furthermore, Saul's family must have owned property and had some importance in the Gentile community as well, for Saul was born not only a citizen of Tarsus (see Acts 21:39) but also of Rome (see Acts 22:27-28).[3]

Saul's parents had such aspirations that they sent their son to study Jewish law in Jerusalem under the foremost rabbi of the day, the Pharisee Gamaliel (see Acts 22:3; Galatians 1:14). The Pharisees (the Hebrew word means "the separated ones") felt that God had set them apart to live by the *Torah* (the Law, or Teaching, of Moses). For them, this meant following the interpretations of the *Torah* laid down by generations of teachers. Some Pharisees held that a man was righteous if he had done more good than bad, but Saul apparently followed the stricter group who insisted that even the least implications of the Law must be kept.[4]

The Pharisees expected a *Messiah* (Hebrew for "Anointed One"; Greek: Christ) who would deliver them from oppression and rule with justice. However, Jesus of Nazareth had infuriated many Pharisees by interpreting the *Torah* differently and claiming a special relationship with God. Thus, when some Jews began to proclaim Jesus as Messiah and Lord (a term usually reserved for God), strict Pharisees opposed them vehemently.

Saul helped lead the fight against the proclaimers of Christ in Jerusalem (see Acts 7:58–8:3; Galatians 1:13). When some were driven out, Saul obtained permission to pursue them to Damascus. But on the way there, Jesus confronted Saul in a blinding encounter (see Acts 9:1-19), revealing to Saul that he was persecuting the very God he professed to worship. From then on, Saul's understanding of God and the *Torah* began to change dramatically. He joined those Jews who were urging other Jews to believe in Jesus, and after some years God called him to proclaim Jesus as Savior to the Gentiles also. Saul took the Greek name "Paul" when he turned to work among Gentiles.

Paul the missionary

Paul spent ten years in the Roman provinces of Cilicia and Syria (see Galatians 1:21), probably preaching Jesus along with Greek-speaking Jewish Christians. Then a believer named Barnabas called him to Syrian Antioch, where by this time rapid conversions had made the church more Gentile than Jewish.[5] After

11

a while, the church in Antioch commissioned Paul and Barnabas to evangelize the provinces of Cyprus and Galatia. The two men succeeded in founding
churches in several cities. Indeed, the mission to the Gentiles was so successful
that the apostles in Jerusalem invited Paul and Barnabas to a council to clarify
exactly what God expected of Gentile believers (see Acts 15). Paul asserted that
both Gentiles and Jews were reconciled to God by faith in Jesus, apart from
keeping the *Torah*, but certain Jews felt that Gentiles must keep all the Jewish
laws. The council confirmed Paul's view of the gospel but his opponents continued to preach against him. Twelve years later, Paul was still fighting those
ideas as they were being put forth in Colosse.

Paul spent the eight years following the council in Jerusalem planting
more churches. He spent more than two of those years building a church
in Ephesus, the queen city of the Roman province of Asia. Then he left the
firmly grounded Ephesian believers to evangelize neighboring cities. Three of
them were Colosse, Laodicea, and Hierapolis in the Lycus River valley, about
a hundred miles east of Ephesus.

In AD 57 Paul brought a charitable gift from his Gentile converts to the
poor believers in Jerusalem. There the Jewish leaders had him arrested as
a blasphemer and a provoker of disorder. He was held pending trial for two
years in Caesarea. Then he appealed for a hearing before the Emperor and
was sent to Rome. After awaiting trial in Rome for another two years, he
was finally released. Sometime during his imprisonment either in Caesarea
or Rome, Paul received a visitor from the strife-torn church in Colosse who
prompted him to write to the believers there.

The town and church of Colosse

Once spoken of as "a great city of Phrygia,"[6] Colosse was, by Paul's time, a
small cosmopolitan city in the province of Asia. Originally known for its wool
industry, the town had declined considerably in importance and had been sur-
passed by Laodicea, ten miles to the west, and Hierapolis, twelve miles to the
northwest (see Colossians 2:1; 4:13,15-16).[7]

The church at Colosse, composed mostly of Gentiles, was not planted by
Paul himself, but most likely by Epaphras, one of his converts at Ephesus.
Although Paul says that he had not been to the church, he had heard of
their faith (see Colossians 1:4). Epaphras seems to have regarded the church
as falling under Paul's missionary jurisdiction, which would have provided
ample reason for him to personally seek out Paul's advice.[8]

Epaphras brought the gospel to Colosse, where it flourished until false
teachers arrived. These men confused young believers by trying to mix ideas
from pagan cults with the gospel. Unable to drive out these wolves alone,
Epaphras appealed to Paul for help. Paul could not go to Colosse personally
because he was in prison, but he could write a letter with all the authority
and wisdom of an apostle to help the Colossian believers see the truth.

The occasion of this letter may have provided an excuse—though an
important one—for Epaphras to visit Paul and to encourage him. Even as
he sought assistance to deal with the convincing arguments and assumed

humility of the leaders of the false teachers, Epaphras brought good news of the progress of the gospel in the Lycus valley.[9]

The heresy

Because Paul only alludes to their doctrines, we may have a hard time figuring out precisely what the false teachers were saying.[10] However, we can make some educated guesses from what Paul criticizes and encourages. Some of the false doctrines were:[11]

1. *Ceremonialism*. There were "strict rules about the kinds of permissible food and drink, religious festivals (see 2:16-17) and circumcision (see 2:11; 3:11)."

2. *Asceticism*. Rules that Paul summarizes as, "Do not handle! Do not taste! Do not touch!" (2:21) and "harsh treatment of the body" (2:23) were supposed to achieve purity.

3. *Angel worship*. See 2:18.

4. *Deprecation of Christ*. Paul stressed Christ's supremacy (see 1:15-20; 2:2-3,9) against those who taught that Christ was on the level of a created angel.

5. *Secret knowledge*. Salvation required not just faith in Christ but knowledge of certain mysteries (see 2:3,18).

6. *Reliance on human wisdom and tradition*. See 2:4,8.

These elements seem to be drawn from "an extreme form of Judaism"[12] and from pagan ideas that later became a system called "Gnosticism" (from the Greek word *gnosis*, "knowledge").

A bit of this, a bit of that

Mixing Greek and oriental ideas and practices was so popular in the first century that we have a word for it: *syncretism*.[13] Everybody wanted to mix his or her own blend of Greek, Roman, Persian, Egyptian, and other doctrines to suit personal taste. Judaism had already absorbed many Greek ideas, and when Gentiles embraced Christianity, they naturally wanted to mix their former beliefs and customs with their new faith.

By the time the Colossian church was established, a pattern was beginning to emerge among the religious recipes being mixed throughout the Empire. We call this semi-standard recipe "Gnosticism," although it was not standardized enough to be called that until the second century AD.

The Gnostics borrowed from at least four areas of tradition: the philosophy of Plato, oriental religion, Judaism, and Christianity. It was perhaps the "borrowing" from Christianity that was most disturbing to Paul, as those who brought such teaching were not just looking for listeners, but for converts.

Among the teachings of the Gnostics were:

1. *The material world is essentially evil* or, at best, indifferent. If the material world is evil, then the body is evil. The body must be kept in place, then, by rigorously holding it in check.[14] How does one do this? "Do not

handle! Do not taste! Do not touch!" (2:21). Paul probably was quoting from the catchwords of the false teachers.[15]

2. *Between God and matter lie a host of fallen (evil) spiritual powers who now rule the world.* Jesus was the first of these rulers; He rules along side other spiritual powers, such as the constellations named in the signs of the Zodiac and the angels. Therefore, He is only one of many bridges to God.

3. *Some human beings possess a divine spark, an inner self that is different from the soul* (the Gnostics were these human beings, of course). This inner self is the true home of such people, which they may reach through a mystical knowledge, a true seeing and hearing.

4. *Redemption is ultimately dependent on the individual's self-understanding* and the resulting freedom it provides, rather than on God.[16] Hence the emphasis on knowledge of secrets rather than on faith.

1. A. T. Robertson, "Paul, the Apostle," *The International Standard Bible Encyclopaedia*, vol. 4 (Grand Rapids, MI: Eerdmans, 1956), 2276.
2. F. F. Bruce, *Paul: Apostle of the Heart Set Free* (Grand Rapids, MI: Eerdmans, 1977), 41–43.
3. Bruce, 32–40.
4. Bruce, 50–52.
5. Bruce, 127–133.
6. Peter O'Brien, *Colossians, Philemon* (Waco, TX: Word, 1982), xxvi.
7. O'Brien, xxvi.
8. Donald Guthrie, *New Testament Introduction* (Downers Grove, IL: InterVarsity, 1970), 545.
9. Guthrie, 546.
10. Guthrie, 546.
11. Kenneth Barker, ed., *The NIV Study Bible* (Grand Rapids, MI: Zondervan, 1985), 1811.
12. Barker, 1811.
13. Herbert M. Carson, *The Epistles of Paul to the Colossians and Philemon* (London: Tyndale, 1960), 15–16.
14. H. Dermot McDonald, *Commentary on Colossians and Philemon* (Waco, TX: Word, 1982), 13.
15. O'Brien, xxxii.
16. Allen C. Myers, ed., "Gnosticism," *The Eerdmans Bible Dictionary* (Grand Rapids, MI: Eerdmans, 1987), 421–423.

OVERVIEW OF COLOSSIANS

A biblical epistle is at once two seemingly contradictory things. It is a letter from a man to a group of people in a particular time and place, and it is a message from the Spirit of God to all Christians in every generation. Just as Christ was fully human and fully divine, so is the letter to the Colossians. In the first part of this overview and in other lessons, we will look at the book mainly from its human side in order to make observations and interpretations. When we get to application, we will focus on the letter's divineness. But before you begin to study, acknowledge the book's supernatural origin by asking the Holy Spirit to speak to you personally and transform you as you study.

This overview will probably take you more time than any other lesson of the study. If necessary, allow one week to read the "How to Use This Study" section, the historical background, and the whole letter to the Colossians. Then take a second week to answer the overview questions.

First impressions

Even though Paul had never been to the church at Colosse, some of its members had been converted through his evangelistic ministry. Among them was Epaphras, who led the church, and Philemon—the owner of the slave Onesimus—in whose house the church may have met. So it was

Optional Application:
Consider how Paul's attitude toward the Colossians might have affected how willingly they received his instruction. How do you think your own attitudes toward others have affected how they responded to your correction? What might you learn from Paul's example?

not to total strangers that Paul wrote, but brothers and sisters whose salvation had been shaped by men and women he knew and trusted. People like Epaphras and Philemon were devoted to Paul and must have conveyed their attitudes to the rest of the church. Now there was confusion among the believers, and in Paul's letter they received authoritative instruction on the issues about which they had questions. They probably read through the letter quickly at first, just to discover Paul's attitude and tone, then went back later to dig out the details.

In the same way, read through the entire letter to the Colossians at one sitting. You may want to read it aloud, as it was read to the Colossians, imagining a cluster of listeners around you. Gather a general impression of Paul's themes and tone.

1. How would you describe the *tone* Paul conveys in this letter? What is his approach to the church at Colosse, their lifestyles, and problems?

   _____

   _____

   _____

   _____

   _____

   _____

   _____

   _____

2. Paul did not hesitate to repeat himself when he wanted to stress a point. What words and ideas are repeated in each of the following sets of verses?

   1:15-18; 3:10 _____

   _____

   _____

   1:18-19; 2:9-10,19; 3:11 _____

   _____

   _____

16

1:9-10,26-28; 2:2-3; 3:10,16; 4:3 _____

_____

_____

2:11; 3:5,10,12,14 _____

_____

_____

other _____

_____

_____

For Thought and Discussion: What clues do you find about Paul's circumstances when he wrote this letter? What clues do you discover regarding the situation at Colosse?

Broad outline

If you are still vague about Paul's intentions after one reading, a broad outline of Colossians may help sharpen your perceptions.

3. Reread Colossians, preferably in a different translation without subheads. You may discover a turn of phrase or word that makes a confusing passage clearer.

   This time, think of a short phrase or sentence that can serve as a title for each paragraph. You may want to include key words from the paragraph. Write your titles below.

   (Be creative. There is no one right answer; the first title is given as an example. Your Bible's paragraph divisions may differ, so feel free to alter those given here.)

   1:1-2 *Greetings to the Faithful*

   1:3-8 _____

   _____

   1:9-14 _____

   _____

   1:15-23 _____

   _____

17

1:24–2:5 _____

_____

2:6-15 _____

_____

2:16-23 _____

_____

3:1-4 _____

_____

3:5-11 _____

_____

3:12-17 _____

_____

3:18–4:1 _____

_____

4:2-6 _____

_____

4:7-18 _____

_____

Theme and purpose

We cannot completely reconstruct the reasons for Paul's letter to the Colossians, but the better we recreate the context, the better we will understand his message. Certainly, like other letter writers, he was responding to what he knew of his readers and their situation. He also wrote from his personal experiences, the track record he had established through his years in the faith and in ministry.

Our own purposes for studying Colossians are separated from those of the original readers by centuries of change, but how we understand and apply his words should be influenced by how the Holy Spirit intended them in the context of the first century.

4. From your first readings of Colossians, what
   seem to be Paul's main reasons for writing this
   letter?

   _____

   _____

   _____

   _____

   _____

   _____

   _____

5. If you have not yet done so, read the historical
   background.

6. Have you come across questions you'd like
   answered as you go deeper into this study? While
   your thoughts are still fresh, you may want to
   record your questions here to serve as personal
   goals for your investigation of the letter.

   _____

   _____

   _____

   _____

   _____

   _____

For Thought and Discussion: If you had to file this letter for later reference, what would you write on the file folder label in addition to "Colossians"?

Study Skill — Application

James 1:22 and 2 Timothy 3:16-17 remind us of the primary reason we study God's Word — to let it affect our lives so that we will become fully the people God desires. Therefore, the last step of Bible study should always be to ask yourself, "What is God saying to me? What difference should this passage make to my life? How should it make me want to think or act?" Application will require time, thought, prayer, and perhaps even discussion with another person.

At times you may find it most productive to concentrate on one specific application giving it careful thought and prayer. At other times you may want to list many implications a passage of Scripture has for your life, meditating on them all for several days before you choose one for concentrated prayer and action. Use whatever method helps you to take to heart and act on what the passage says.

7. The letter to the Colossians was written to a specific church at a specific point in history, but it is also God's Word to us today. As you read through Colossians, did you find areas that might apply to you? If so, what are some of those areas?

_____

_____

_____

_____

_____

8. Summarize what is to you the most significant first impression from your study so far.

_____

_____

_____

_____

_____

20

For the group

This "For the group" section and the ones in later lessons are intended to suggest ways of structuring your discussions. Feel free to select and adapt what suits your group. The main goals of this lesson are to get to know Colossians as a whole and the people with whom you are going to study it.

Worship. Colossians is an excellent setting for focusing on worship together. Some passages sound like hymns the Colossians might have sung in their own worship (see 1:15-20; 2:9-15), and Paul urges the Colossians to sing "psalms, hymns, and songs from the Spirit, singing to God with gratitude in your hearts" (3:16). Because the false teachers denigrated Christ, this letter encourages believers to glorify Him. Take some time to focus on Christ by singing a psalm, hymn, or spiritual song together. Even reading a psalm together, such as Psalms 24, 92, 96, 97, 98, 99, or 100, will help you center your hearts on God.

Warm-up. The beginning of a new study is a good time to lay a foundation for honest sharing of ideas, to get comfortable with each other, and to encourage a sense of common purpose. Talk about what each member hopes to get out of your group—out of your study of Colossians and out of any prayer, singing, sharing, outreach, or anything else you might do together. Why do you want to study the Bible? If you have someone write down each member's hopes and expectations, then you can look back at these goals later to see if they are being met. Allow about ten minutes for this discussion.

How to use this study. If the group has never used a LifeChange study guide before, you might take a whole meeting to get acquainted, discuss your backgrounds and goals for the study, and go over the "How to Use This Study" section. Then you can take a second meeting to discuss the background and the overview questions. This will give you more time to read Colossians and prepare lesson 1 for discussion.

It is a good idea to clear up any confusion about how to do the study as soon as possible, so at the beginning of your second meeting, ask the group if anyone was confused about how to do lesson 1.

Optional Application: Read 2 Timothy 2:9 and Hebrews 4:12. How do you think the nature of God's Word helps you apply it to contemporary life? How might that perspective affect how you study the book of Colossians?

21

Reading. It is often helpful to refresh everyone's memory by reading the passage aloud before beginning to discuss your lesson. Reading the whole letter may take time, but the effort will be rewarded. Have a different person read each chapter, using the tone of voice he or she thinks Paul was trying to convey so that the letter sounds like the work of a living person. It should take perhaps fifteen minutes to read all of Colossians.

First impressions. Ask the group to share first impressions of Colossians—its style, mood, content, or whatever strikes the group. If members don't understand the question, you might ask them how Paul's letter is like and unlike letters they receive, or like and unlike a sermon, a graduation speech, or advice from a parent. The point of question 1 is to help the group see Colossians as a letter from a real person to real people for a specific occasion. Don't spend more than a few minutes on this question.

The setting of the letter is an important part of its context. The background may help you to understand the setting. Ask several group members to tell who Paul was, what is important to know about the Colossians, and what was going on in Paul's and the Colossians' lives when he wrote. By piecing together everyone's recollections of the background, you can probably recall the main points. Then, using the background and clues from the letter, see how much you can conclude about why Paul was writing and what was going on at the time.

To help the group get to know Paul as a real person, ask them to share what kind of person they think he was (based on the background and the letter). Application will require you to put yourselves in Paul's shoes, and it will be easier to identify with him if he seems real to you.

Looking for repeated words and ideas (question 2) should help the group see themes and main ideas in the letter. You might ask the group to name as many repeated phrases and ideas as possible, then move to question 4 on the letter's themes. You could share your titles (question 3) after that. Remember, there is no one right way to title a passage.

Questions. Give everyone a chance to share questions about the letter or the way you are studying it. It is good to clear up confusion about the book, the group, or the study guide as early as possible. You may want to leave some questions about the book until later in your study; they may answer themselves. You may point out the list of references or encourage members to seek answers from their pastors or other knowledgeable Christians they respect.

Application. Question 7 ties in with the expectations and objectives you discussed at the beginning of your meeting. If some group members are unfamiliar with how to apply God's Word to their lives in specific ways, this is a chance to think of some sample applications together. (You could do this next week if you are running out of time.) Application is often the most difficult part of the study because many people have never been taught how to apply Scripture consciously, yet it is essential to the Christian life.

Wrap-up. The group leader should have read through lesson 2 and its "For the group" section. At this point, he or she might give a short summary of what members can expect in that lesson and in the coming meeting. This is a chance to whet everyone's appetite, assign any optional questions, omit any numbered questions, or forewarn members of any possible difficulties.

You might also encourage any members who found the overview especially hard. Some people are better at seeing the big picture or the whole of a book than others. Some are best at analyzing a particular verse or paragraph, while others are strongest at seeing how a passage applies to our lives. Urge members to give thanks for their own and others' strengths, and to give and request help when needed. The group is a place to learn from each other. Later lessons will draw on the gifts of close analyzers as well as overviewers and appliers, practical as well as theoretical thinkers.

Worship. Many groups like to end with singing and/or prayer. This can include songs and prayers that respond to what you've learned in Colossians or prayers for specific needs of group members. Many people are shy about sharing personal needs or praying aloud in groups, especially before they know the other people well. If this is true of your group, then a song and/or some silent prayer, and a short closing prayer spoken by the leader might be

23

an appropriate end. You could share requests and pray in pairs, instead, if you prefer.

1. David L. Thompson, *Bible Study That Works* (Grand Rapids, MI: Francis Asbury Press, 1982), 28.

COLOSSIANS 1:1-14
Thanks and Concerns

As was customary in ancient letters, Paul begins by identifying first the senders, then the recipients (see 1:1-2). He follows with a greeting (see 1:2) and continues by listing the reasons he is thankful to God for the Colossian church (see 1:3-8). He reminds the Colossians how he prays for them, demonstrating his sensitivity to their needs (see 1:9-14). This is not simply a cushion for the harder instruction to come, but an expression of encouragement for the past and hopes for the future. Read 1:1-14, asking God to teach you how Paul prayed.

Greetings to the faithful (1:1-2)

Apostle (1:1). The Greek word *apostolos* means "one who is sent." The New Testament apostle is not just a delivery service, but an authoritative messenger of God (see John 20:21). Because Paul's readers do not know him personally, he wants them to understand that he speaks by command of Christ.

Holy (1:2). "Saints" in NASB, meaning "set apart ones." They are not yet perfect, but they are living holy lives, having been made holy by Christ.

Grace (1:2). The normal Greek greeting was *charein*, meaning "greetings" or "favor from me

25

to you." Paul preferred a related word, *charis*, which named God's favor bestowed on sinful individuals with no strings attached. This greeting is a prayer, then, that they may enjoy the blessing of God Himself.[1]

Peace (1:2). This was the common Jewish greeting. It meant wholeness and well-being in all aspects of life—health, harmony between people, a flourishing earth, and so on. To wish someone peace was to wish him or her a foretaste of the Messianic Age foretold by the prophets, a taste of God's presence and the fulfillment that flows from that presence.[2]

1. Paul identifies himself as an "apostle" and Timothy and the Colossians as his "brothers." What do these words tell you about the relationship Paul felt he had with the Colossians whom he had never seen?

_____

_____

_____

_____

_____

Thanks to God (1:3-8)

Faith (1:4-5). When the gospel has been heard and understood, the result is faith—full confidence, trust, belief that Jesus is the Son of God (see Romans 10:17). Faith is demonstrated by obedience (see Romans 1:5).

Love (1:4-5). As with faithfulness, love is one of the fruits of a right relationship with God (see Galatians 5:22-23). Love among Christian brothers and sisters was to be their trademark (see John 13:35; 1 John 3:23). For this reason, Paul calls it "the greatest" of the Christian character trio—faith, hope, and love (see 1 Corinthians 13:13).

26

Hope (1:5). "Not wishful thinking, but a firm assurance."[3] This certainty is based on God's promises of Christ's return, of the resurrection of the body, and of eternal life.[4]

The truth . . . the gospel (1:5-6). These terms are interchangeable. The gospel—God's Word spoken and revealed to individuals—is the truth. Paul contrasts the truth found in the gospel with "hollow and deceptive philosophy" (2:8).

For Further Study: The relationship of faith, hope, and love is expanded elsewhere in Scripture. Compare Colossians 1:4-5 with one or more of the following: Romans 5:1-5; 1 Corinthians 13:13; Ephesians 4:1-6; 1 Thessalonians 1:3; 5:8; Hebrews 6:10-12.

2. Paul expresses his thanks for the believers at Colosse because of their faith, love, and hope (1:4-5). Observe how these graces are expressed in their lives. What do you learn from 1:3-8 about . . .

faith? _____

_____

_____

_____

love? _____

_____

_____

hope? _____

_____

_____

_____

3. Why is it crucial that our hope is stored up in heaven (see 1:5)?

_____

_____

_____

_____

4. What does it mean to have "love in the Spirit" (1:8)?

_____

_____

_____

_____

5. What reasons do you have to thank God for the community of faith (church, fellowship, small group) of which you are a part?

_____

_____

_____

_____

_____

6. Paul says the gospel, the word of truth, is already "bearing fruit and growing" all over the world (1:6). What was necessary before the gospel could bear fruit and grow within the Colossians (see 1:6)?

_____

_____

_____

_____

7. What do you think "bearing fruit and growing" means in this context? (*Optional*: See Mark 4:1-20.)

_____

_____

_____

_____

_____

8. How has the gospel been bearing fruit and growing in you since you first heard and understood it?

_____

_____

_____

_____

Concerns for completeness (1:9-14)

Wisdom and understanding (1:9). True wisdom and understanding find their source in God and are revealed by the Holy Spirit. They do not grow from human reasoning, but from "the fear of the LORD" (Proverbs 9:10).

Worthy (1:10). The phrase "worthy of the Lord" is a formula similar to one that appeared on inscriptions dedicated to pagan gods in the province of Asia. We might say, "so as to satisfy him in all respects."[5]

Strengthened . . . power . . . might (1:11). The repetition of the synonyms shows how difficult it is to express the fullness of God's power in words. The expressions that Paul uses here are common in early Christian doxologies (literally, "words of praise") that praise God for His glory and power.[6] The word used for "power," _kratos_, in the New Testament is used only of God. His power becomes our strength.[7]

Qualified (1:12). Made fit or competent, as when an athlete is qualified to compete.

9. a. Break down the complicated sentences in Colossians 1:9-10 by completing the following phrases. Paul and Timothy continue to pray for the Colossians, asking God . . .

to fill them with _____

_____

Optional Application: Think of a Christian you know who has encouraged you by his or her act of faith, hope, or love. Make a point to express your thanks to him or her by a similar deed, as you think God would have you do so.

For Thought and Discussion: How does God go about building spiritual wisdom into us when we pray for it? Does He sometimes just drop it into our brains? Does He sometimes send painful experiences to teach us wisdom? What does wisdom cost us?

Optional Application:
a. Plan to pray daily this week for the knowledge of God's will through spiritual wisdom and understanding. Pray for this help to live a life worthy of the Lord.

b. What other steps can you take to bear fruit in good works and grow in personal knowledge of God (not just knowledge about Him)?

For Thought and Discussion: How does Paul's definition of a life that is pleasing to God compare with the list of the fruit of the Spirit in Galatians 5:22-23? How does one passage help you understand the other?

through all _____

_____

in order that _____

_____

b. What do they pray will be the outgrowth of their request (see 1:10)?

_____

_____

_____

10. a. How does Paul say the Colossians will know they are pleasing God (see 1:10-12)?

_____

_____

_____

_____

b. In light of these verses, how can you know when you are pleasing God and being fruitful?

_____

_____

_____

11. a. What do you think Paul means by "the inheritance of his holy people" (1:12)? (*Optional*: See Romans 8:16-23.)

_____

_____

_____

_____

_____

b. When have or will the Colossians share in this inheritance?

_____

_____

_____

_____

Study Skill — Contrast and Compare
When summarizing a passage, look for ideas, phrases, or people that show contrasts or points of comparison. For example, in Proverbs, the wise person and the foolish person are contrasted because they are so different. In John 10, Jesus is compared with a good shepherd because He is so much like a good shepherd.

As you study Colossians you may ask questions like, "How is the old life different from the new?" and "How is a life that is pleasing to God like a fruitful tree?"

---

12. a. How is the "dominion of darkness" different from "the kingdom of the Son" (1:13-14)? (*Optional*: See Romans 6:15-23; Ephesians 2:1-7; 4:17-24.)

_____

_____

_____

_____

_____

b. How does your experience compare with the experience of the Colossians in 1:13-14?

_____

_____

_____

Optional Application: Each day this week, take time to thank God for qualifying you to share in the inheritance of the Kingdom of light. How can you express your gratitude in deeds as well?

For Thought and Discussion: What other ideas or phrases can you think of that show the contrast in Colossians 1:12-14? Note especially concepts from the Bible, but don't stop there.

31

Optional Application: Review the reasons Paul was thankful to God for the Colossians. How might he have expressed his thankfulness differently and similarly if he had been writing to you?

For Further Study: How is the phrasing in Colossians 1:13-14 similar to that in Mark 1:4,11,15; Luke 24:46-47; and Acts 10:43-44?

13. What one truth in 1:1-14 has implications for your life that you would like to concentrate on for application? (Ask God to give you wisdom to discern this.)

_____

_____

_____

_____

_____

14. What action can you take this week to put this truth into practice in a new way?

_____

_____

_____

15. Write down any questions that have arisen during your study.

_____

_____

_____

_____

For the group

Worship. Songs of thanksgiving, especially those focused on fruitfulness and our liberation from darkness, would be appropriate for this lesson. A song that is usually reserved for the Thanksgiving holiday might gain new meaning for you if you sing it in the context of Colossians 1:6,10. Or, Exodus 15:1-18 and Psalm 114 celebrate Israel's rescue from Egypt, the foreshadow of our rescue from darkness (see Colossians 1:12-14). You might let someone read one of these praise songs aloud.

Warm-up. To further help everyone move from the day's busyness to the topic of Colossians 1:1-14, ask a simple warm-up question. For example, ask everyone to share what he or she is most thankful to God for today.

Summarize. It is a good idea to glance at the forest before examining each tree. Let someone briefly summarize what 1:1-14 is about. What are the common threads that run through the passage?

Questions. As you study each paragraph, keep thinking of how what Paul is saying applies to you as an individual in God's family of faith. Some of the questions ask for specific applications, while the "Optional Application" questions are even more direct. The questions stress the idea of fruitfulness, but you can choose another emphasis.

If the group members know one another well, you might let them take turns telling what fruit they have seen in each other's lives during the past few months. Then let each person tell what aspect of 1:1-14 he or she wants to apply, and how. If some of you are having trouble deciding how to apply something you've learned, you might discuss some suggestions together.

Summarize. To wrap up your discussion, let someone summarize again what 1:1-14 is about and repeat some of the ways in which group members plan to apply the passage.

Worship. Conclude your time together with a prayer of thanks for the fruit being produced in the group members. The group leader may pray, or individuals may wish to thank God for specific good works that they have enjoyed from other members. Also, thank God for delivering you from the dominion of darkness and including you in the inheritance of His holy people. Pray for knowledge of God's will, and ask to be strengthened with God's power for endurance.

Optional Application: Review the ways the Colossians could know they were being pleasing to God. What are some specific actions you might take to express your own obedience to God?

For Further Study: Lesson 1, question 3 gave you a head start toward outlining Colossians. To help yourself pull together the main threads of 1:1-14, try outlining the passage. The subtitles in this lesson may help.

1. Herbert M. Carson, *The Epistles of Paul to the Colossians and Philemon* (London: Tyndale, 1960), 29.
2. Hartmut Beck and Colin Brown, "Peace," *The New International Dictionary of New Testament Theology*, vol. 2 (Grand Rapids, MI: Zondervan, 1975), 776–783.

3. Kenneth Barker, ed., *The NIV Study Bible* (Grand Rapids, MI: Zondervan, 1985), 1813.
4. Carson, 31.
5. F. F. Bruce, *The Epistles to the Colossians, to Philemon, and to the Ephesians* (Grand Rapids, MI: Eerdmans, 1984), 46–47.
6. Arthur G. Patzia, *Colossians, Philemon, Ephesians* (San Francisco: Harper & Row, 1984), 9.
7. Carson, 37.

COLOSSIANS 1:15-23

Hymn to Christ

To combat teachers who are reducing Christ to the level of an angel or a subordinate god, Paul not only declares Christ's supremacy—he sings it. Verses 15-20 are written in the poetic rhythm of a hymn. Paul is not telling the Colossians anything new; he is singing what they already believe as a reminder and reinforcement.

Read 1:15-20 aloud to yourself with meaning, as though you were reading the words of a hymn of praise. Then read aloud Paul's explanation of the hymn in 1:21-23. (Reading aloud helps you focus on and absorb the words through sound as well as sight.)

Hymn (1:15-20)

1. What titles and descriptions of Christ do you find in 1:15-20? List as many as possible.

_____

_____

_____

_____

_____

_____

_____

_____

2. This hymn has two stanzas: 1:15-16 and 1:17-20. Make up your own title for the whole song and a title for each stanza.

1:15-20 _____

    1:15-16 _____

    1:17-20 _____

3. Paul wrote this song while under house arrest, a prisoner of the Roman authorities. How is it significant that Paul could declare these words while in this situation?

_____

_____

_____

_____

_____

Image (1:15). This is a deliberate paradox that stretches our minds: Jesus is the visible image of Someone invisible. In Jesus, God provides us with an image—a reflection and revelation—of His true identity. While other symbols in the church show us certain facets of God (like three intertwined circles help us understand the Trinity), only Jesus shows us everything we need to know about God (see John 1:18; 14:9).

Firstborn (1:15). Just like the firstborn son in a Hebrew family, Jesus is the heir to His Father's household and has special privileges and responsibilities. Just as the oldest Hebrew son had authority over his brothers, so Jesus is preeminent over creation. Further, He was the beginning, or founder, of a new spiritual creation (see 1:18).[1]

Thrones or powers or rulers or authorities (1:16). Various grades of angels and spiritual beings, either good or evil. The false teachers apparently put great emphasis on angels (see 2:18).

Head (1:18). This figure of speech meant primarily "source" in Greek (like the head of a river). Just as the head of a body supplies life and manages the body, so Christ is the source and origin of the church's life. The vital spark that animates the whole is Christ's risen life, which He shares with His people.[2] Because "head" means "source," it also implies honor and authority (see 2:10).

Fullness (1:19). All the activities and attributes of God—His Spirit, word, wisdom, and glory—take up their residence (dwell) in Christ.[3]

Reconcile to himself all things (1:20). "When Adam and Eve sinned, not only was the harmony between God and man destroyed, but also disorder came into creation (Romans 8:19-22). So when Christ died on the cross, he made peace possible between God and man, and he restored in principle the harmony in the physical world, though the full realization of the latter will come only when Christ returns (Romans 8:21)."[4]

Study Skill — Application Then and Now
Before thinking how to apply a passage to your own life, consider how its first readers would have done so.[5] In 1:15-20, Paul emphasizes Christ's preeminence. Each statement is a challenge to reject the teachers who reduce Christ and to let Christ be first in the Colossians' lives. Think about how this first-century application helps you apply the passage to yourself.

---

4. Paul uses several words or phrases to explain how Christ is supreme in 1:15-20. Below are some of them. Choose at least two, and write down how they are personally important to you. How should each of them affect your attitudes and actions?

   "The Son is the image of the invisible God" and "God was pleased to have all his fullness dwell in him"

   _____

   _____

37

_____

_____

_____

_____

"all things have been created through him and for him"

_____

_____

_____

_____

"in him all things hold together"

_____

_____

_____

_____

"he is the head of the body, the church"

_____

_____

_____

_____

"God was pleased . . . through him to reconcile to himself all things"

_____

_____

_____

_____

_____

5. What do you think Paul means when he says Christ is "the firstborn from among the dead" (1:18)? (*Optional*: See 1 Corinthians 15:12-23.)

_____

_____

_____

_____

_____

Optional Application: Think of a good Christian friend. How does he or she reflect God's image? How does Christ reflect God more completely than your friend?

6. How does Colossians 1:19-20 help to explain the way in which Christ reflects . . .

God's image?_____

_____

_____

_____

_____

_____

_____

God's purposes? _____

_____

_____

_____

_____

_____

Optional Application: How did your behavior change when you came to faith in Christ? If you came to faith very early in life, in what ways have you seen God help you grow and endure in the faith?

Explanation (1:21-23)

7. In 1:21-23, Paul shows how the new lives of the Colossians differ radically from their old ones. What changes have occurred . . .

in their relationships with God?

old	new

in their behavior?

old	new

8. How were these changes made possible (see 1:19-20,22)?

_____

_____

40

_____

_____

9. Summarize in one sentence what you learned from this lesson.

_____

_____

_____

_____

10. What one truth in this lesson do you find most significant for you personally?

_____

_____

_____

_____

11. How do you think this truth may help you continue in your faith this week? How should it affect what you think and do?

_____

_____

_____

_____

12. List any questions you have about 1:15-23.

_____

_____

_____

_____

For Thought and Discussion: How does an individual know he or she is continuing in faith (see Colossians 1:23; 1 John 2:3-6; 3:18-20,23-24)?

For Further Study: Add 1:15-23 to your outline, if you are making one.

41

For the group

Worship. In previous sessions the group has prayed and sung together, just as the Colossian Christians did. But as the "Praise to Christ, the First, the Best" box below explains, early Christian worship was patterned on Jewish worship. To get the flavor of what worship might have been like at Colosse, try reading Psalm 29, 45, or 47 aloud together in the same translation. Then sing a song that praises Christ.

Read aloud. Let one member of your group read Colossians 1:15-23. Remind the reader that in the Greek, the passage has the rhythm of a hymn. It should be read joyfully and triumphantly.

Summarize. What is Paul's main point in this passage?

Background notes. This study guide is full of word definitions and comments on the text. Don't get bogged down in these; you don't have to learn it all. Feel free to discuss and/or disagree with the notes. When alternate interpretations are given, you might discuss which view convinces you.

Questions. Never feel that you must cover all the questions in a Bible study lesson just because they are in the book. You can focus on one or two concepts, or ignore the numbered questions and discuss some optional questions that interest you. You probably can't adequately cover all the numbered and optional questions, so take time before each group meeting to select which ones you want to discuss.

Summarize.

Worship. At the end of your meeting, save time to offer spontaneous praise to Christ, using Colossians 1:15-23 as a springboard. Thank God for what He has done, and praise Jesus for who He is.

Praise to Christ, the First, the Best
Imagine Saul of Tarsus worshiping God. From his childhood, he had worshiped in his family's synagogue. Morning, noon, and night,

---

42

wherever he found himself, he said the *Shemoneh 'Esreh*, the Hebrew intercession for the righteous within the community of Israel.[6] These prayers, songs, hymns, and confessions were as familiar to him as "Jesus loves me. This I know . . ." or "Holy, holy, holy, Lord God Almighty . . ." are to us.

Then Saul converted to Christ and became Paul. Did he leave his lifelong worship habits behind, the prayers rich with praise and thanksgiving, the confessions thick with repentance? Did he no longer pray three times a day?

Probably, like other Christians, Paul continued to pray three times a day, now incorporating Matthew 6:9-13 and new Christian prayers into his worship. Like Jesus, who had followed the synagogal pattern of prayer, Paul created or rewrote prayers intended to be spoken aloud, filling them with the completeness of Christ.

In the early days of Christianity, believers met in the synagogue on Sabbaths, and on ordinary weekdays they held informal prayer meetings in private homes. On the first day of the week, they may have held a special form of worship, including the "breaking of bread" — the Lord's Supper.

One of the oldest prayers of the nation of Israel, *'Alenu* prayer, begins:

"It is meet that we should praise the Lord of all; that we should ascribe greatness to Him who formed (the world) from the beginning."

The prayer continues: "They worship vain things and emptiness; they pray unto that which profiteth not.

"We worship before the King of the kings of kings; that stretcheth out the heavens and layeth the foundation of the earth . . .

"He is our God, and there is none other beside; truly our King, and there is none but He."[7]

What are the parallels in this prayer with Paul's hymn of praise in Colossians 1:15-20? We can see that he was not so much giving the Colossians new information as he was reminding them, from their own traditions, that Christ, Son of the King of the kings of kings, reigns supreme.

(continued on page 44)

43

(continued from page 43)

The false teachers in Colosse were in part trying to draw the Christians into Jewish practices that negated the gospel (see 2:16-17). Yet Paul used the familiar Jewish-Christian form of hymn to affirm the gospel. He was able to distinguish which parts of the Jewish tradition were to be laid aside, and which parts could be adapted to enrich Christian life.

1. Peter O'Brien, *Colossians, Philemon* (Waco, TX: Word, 1982), 50–51; Kenneth Barker, ed., *The NIV Study Bible* (Grand Rapids, MI: Zondervan, 1985), 1814.
2. F. F. Bruce, *The Epistles to the Colossians, to Philemon, and to the Ephesians* (Grand Rapids, MI: Eerdmans, 1984), 68.
3. O'Brien, 53.
4. Barker, 1814.
5. James F. Nyquist, *Leading Bible Discussions* (Downers Grove, IL: InterVarsity, 1967), 32.
6. W. O. E. Oesterley, *The Jewish Background of the Christian Liturgy* (Gloucester, MA: Peter Smith, 1965), 53.
7. Oesterley, 68.

COLOSSIANS 1:24–2:5

Hard Work for Christ

"How do I explain how much I care for you, even though we've never met?" Is this a question from a romance novel? No, it is Paul's own desire to demonstrate his pastoral care and compassion, even for a congregation he had not personally met. Their conversion occurred, in part, because of his hard work in the past. Now he wants them to know how much he continues to struggle on their behalf. By explaining how he has suffered, he is better able to express his sympathy for their own struggles.

Before you begin your study of 1:24–2:5, review quickly 1:15-23, noting the prevalent themes. Also review the title you gave to 1:24–2:5 in lesson 1. Now read the passage through, using several translations, if possible.

Stewardship of a secret (1:24-29)

Servant (1:23,25). "Minister" in NASB. To Gentiles, a servant was a menial worker. In the Old Testament, a servant was a trusted minister or envoy of a king.[1] The apostles saw that their mission was to represent Jesus, who by His obedience fulfilled what was written about God's Servant (see Isaiah 42:1-9; 49:1-7; 52:13–53:12). In Colossians, Paul calls himself God's servant to show how the mission of the individual Suffering Servant has been extended to all of God's people.[2]

45

What I am suffering for you (1:24). For the sake
of those who needed to hear the gospel, Paul
endured beatings, imprisonment, and other
hardships that he names in 2 Corinthians
11:23-33.

***Fill up in my flesh what is still lacking in regard
to Christ's afflictions*** (1:24). This "does not
mean that there was a deficiency in the atoning
sacrifice of Christ. Rather, it means that Paul
suffered afflictions because he was preaching
the good news of Christ's atonement. Christ
suffered on the cross to atone for sin, and Paul
filled up Christ's afflictions by experiencing the
added sufferings necessary to carry this good
news to a lost world."[3]

Mystery (1:26-27; 2:2). A concealed truth known only
to God and that only He may reveal and interpret.[4] Pagan cults (and possibly the false teachers
in Colosse) spoke of mysteries as exclusive information they alone possessed, but Paul says that
the true mystery of Christ "is now disclosed to
the Lord's people" and "among the Gentiles."

---

1. To communicate his care for the Colossians,
   Paul says a lot about his own mission in 1:24-29.
   How does he describe his mission?

   1:24 _____

   _____

   _____

   1:25 _____

   _____

   _____

   1:28 _____

   _____

   _____

   _____

2. a. Paul says, "I fill up in my flesh what is still
      lacking in regard to Christ's afflictions" (1:24).
      Do you think this was true only of the apostles
      or is it true of God's servants today? Why?

   _____

   _____

   _____

   _____

   _____

   b. Do you desire to be a servant who participates
      in the suffering to bring news of Christ to a
      lost world? Why or why not?

   _____

   _____

   _____

   _____

   _____

3. a. Verse 24 shows how intimately Christ and
      His church are connected. How are they
      connected?

   _____

   _____

   _____

   b. According to 1:24, how does Paul model this
      intimate connection between Christ and His
      people?

   _____

   _____

   _____

For Further Study:
Skim Daniel 2:31-45.
How does this pattern for revealing a mystery compare with the pattern in Colossians 1:25-27?

Optional Application: Have you ever been told a wonderful secret that no one else knew? How did you feel, knowing you were the only one who knew? How did you feel when you were finally able to tell others the secret?

4. Paul's mission is to proclaim the mystery that has been hidden (see 1:25-27).

   a. What is the mystery?

   _____

   _____

   b. What do you think this means? (Explain in your own words.)

   _____

   _____

   _____

   _____

   c. How long has the mystery been hidden?

   _____

   _____

   d. To whom has it been revealed?

   _____

   _____

Fully mature (1:28). Members of pagan mystery religions (and possibly the false teachers) called "perfect" those who had received their special secrets or knowledge. In Christ, however, every believer is as perfect as a newborn baby without blemishes. Yet, the newborn believer must still mature to his or her full potential and work out the overcoming of his or her sinful nature (see Philippians 2:12-13). The Greek word for *perfect* also means "mature" or "complete."

---

5. How does Paul help people become perfect or mature in Christ (see 1:28-29)?

   _____

   _____

6. Even if you are not in a formal teaching or leadership position, what can you do to help Christians around you—in your family, work, church—become more mature in Christ?

_____

_____

_____

_____

Optional Application: Paul says he gets from Christ his energy to proclaim Him. How do you think Paul harnessed this energy? If you are lacking in energy, what do you think God would have you do about it?

7. Why do you think Paul emphasizes that he struggles "with all [Christ's] energy" (1:29)? (*Optional*: See John 15:1-5; 2 Corinthians 4:7; 12:9.)

_____

_____

_____

_____

Struggle for the saints (2:1-5)

8. Paul emphasizes that he "strenuously contend[s]" ("toiling strenuously" in NEB, "striving" in RSV) for the Lord's people at Colosse and at Laodicea (1:29). But he is in prison. In what ways do you think he is exerting himself for them?

_____

_____

_____

_____

Optional Application: Based on Paul's example, how can you struggle with God's energy for your fellow Christians to achieve what Paul describes in 2:2-3?

Optional Application: Think of someone you know who needs to be "encouraged in heart" (2:2). What can you do this week to help him or her? How can your life better reflect the mystery of "Christ in you"(1:27)?

9. What does Paul hope to accomplish through his struggles (see 2:2-3)?

_____

_____

_____

_____

10. Remember from Colossians 1:19 that all the fullness of God dwells — has taken up residence — in Christ. Why is it important to you that *all* the treasures of wisdom and knowledge are hidden in Christ (see 2:3-4)?

_____

_____

_____

_____

11. What do you think are the "fine-sounding arguments" to which Paul is referring in 2:4?

_____

_____

_____

_____

12. Summarize in one or two sentences the theme of 1:24–2:5.

_____

_____

_____

_____

Study Skill — Application

It can be helpful to plan an application in several steps:

1. Record the verse or passage that contains the truth you want to apply to your life. If the passage is short enough, consider copying it word for word, as an aid to memory. (Memorizing the passage is always a good idea, because you can then meditate on it anytime during the day.)

2. State the truth of the passage that impresses you. For instance, *"Even in prison, Paul is struggling with all Christ's strength to present everyone perfect in Christ."*

3. Describe how you already see this truth at work positively in your life. (This is a chance to rejoice in what God is doing.) For example, *"Last week I knew it was Christ speaking His wisdom through me when I talked with Barbara about the situation she is facing."*

4. Tell how you fall short in relation to this truth, or how you want the truth to affect your life. (Ask God to enable you to see yourself clearly.) For example, *"I have a tendency to rely on my own strength and wisdom to give people advice and help, rather than on Jesus'. Also, I am often better at giving biblical counsel than at living it myself. I should be more of a model of Christian maturity, and less of a mouthpiece for it."*

5. State precisely what you plan to do about having your life changed in this area. (Ask God what, if anything, you can do. Don't forget that transformation depends on His will, power, and timing, not on yours. Diligent prayer should always be part of your application.) For instance, *"I'm going to meditate on Colossians 1:28-29 for five or ten minutes each day this week. I'm going to copy those verses and tape them on my desk to remind myself. I'm going to ask God to forgive me for talking better than I live and for trying to do His work in my strength. I'll ask Him also to enable me to see the difference between His strength and mine, and to help me rely on Him. The next time I'm inclined to give someone biblical*

(continued on page 52)

Optional Application: Pray daily this week for Christians you know, using 2:2-3 as a model.

For Further Study: John 1:1-14 explains more about the mystery of the Word, who is God. Read this passage. What similar concepts to Colossians 1:15-19 do you find? To Colossians 1:25-27 and 2:2-3?

For Further Study:
Add 1:24–2:5 to your
outline, if you are
making one.

(continued from page 51)

*counsel, I'm going to take seriously whether I'm
living by it myself."*
    6. Plan a way to remind yourself to do what
you've decided, such as putting a note on your
refrigerator or in your office, or asking a friend
to remind you.[5]

13. What was the most significant truth you
    learned from Colossians 1:24–2:5?

    _____

    _____

    _____

    _____

    _____

14. How do you already see this truth at work in
    your own life?

    _____

    _____

    _____

    _____

    _____

15. How do you fall short or want to grow in this
    area?

    _____

    _____

    _____

    _____

    _____

16. What steps can you take to accomplish this, by God's grace?

_____

_____

_____

_____

_____

17. List any questions you have about 1:24–2:5.

_____

_____

_____

_____

For the group

Warm-up. Ask everyone to remember a time when he or she was told a wonderful secret. Then ask, "How eager were you to pass it on?" The mystery entrusted to Paul is like one of those wonderful secrets.

Worship. You might sing a song or two about servanthood. Or, have someone read aloud Isaiah 49:1-7 or 52:13–53:12 to show what the Servant's mission was.

Read aloud. Read Colossians 1:24–2:5 aloud with meaning.

Summarize.

The mystery and maturity. As you have seen, Paul's goal for the Colossians is that they experience "the full riches of complete understanding" (2:2) of who Christ is. In addition to, or instead of, the questions in the lesson, you might discuss some or all of the following:

What part does each member of your group play in making known the mystery among the

53

Gentiles (see 1:27)? How are you reflecting Christ before non-Christians? Are some of you spreading the gospel by helping other Christians to mature in their faith? How are you accomplishing this? What can you say to each other now to encourage one another in your struggle for Christ? What specifically can you do this week to improve your unity in love?

Is anyone in your group having to deal with "fine-sounding arguments"(2:4)? Discuss the situation, and offer assistance and encouragement. You may know of a book or article that will help, or the individual may simply need to be exhorted to remain firm in his or her faith in Christ.

Summarize.

Worship. Close by thanking God for the participation of group members in spreading the gospel and for spiritual growth within your group. Ask God for guidance for individuals who are being harrassed or tempted with arguments that would lead them away from Christ. Thank Him for His servants who fill up in their flesh what is lacking in Christ's afflictions, and for revealing the mystery of Christ to you.

Someday, When I'm Perfect . . .

In considering Colossians 1:28, William Law wrote on the danger of waiting until we are perfect — or at least "better" — before we start serving the Lord:

"There is no falseness of our hearts that leads us into greater errors than imagining that we shall some time or other be better than we are now. Perfection has no dependence upon external circumstances; it wants no times or opportunities, but it is in its highest state when we are making the best use of that condition in which we are now placed.

"The poor widow did not stay until she was rich before she contributed to the treasury. She readily brought her mite, little as it was, and it got her the reward and commendation of great charity. We must imitate the wisdom of the poor widow and exercise every virtue in the same manner that she exercised her charity. We must stay for no time or opportunities, wait

54

for no change of life or fancied abilities, but remember that every time is a time for piety and perfection.

"Let us not vainly say that if we had lived in the days of our Lord, we would have followed Him, or that if we could work miracles, we would devote ourselves to His glory. To follow Christ as far as we can in our present state and to do all we are able for His glory is as acceptable to Him as if we were working miracles in His name . . .

"We must reckon ourselves no further as living like Christians than we live like Christ."[6]

1. Kenneth Barker, ed., *The NIV Study Bible* (Grand Rapids, MI: Zondervan, 1985), 1076.
2. F. F. Bruce, *The Epistles to the Colossians, to Philemon, and to the Ephesians* (Grand Rapids, MI: Eerdmans, 1984), 82.
3. Barker, 1814.
4. Peter O'Brien, *Colossians, Philemon* (Waco, TX: Word, 1982), 84.
5. This "Five-Point Application" is based on the method in *The 2:7 Series*, Course 4 (Colorado Springs, CO: NavPress, 1979), 50–51.
6. Erwin Randolph, ed., *William Law on Christian Perfection* (Minneapolis: Bethany Fellowship, 1975), 130–131. Originally published in England, titled *Christian Perfection*, in 1726.

COLOSSIANS 2:6-23
Living in Christ

Having made evident the utter completeness of Christ, Paul can go on to point out the flaws in the fine-sounding arguments to which the Colossians have been listening. "My Gentile people are being told they have to celebrate the Jewish religious festivals and abstain from all kinds of things," we can almost hear Epaphras lament. "They're being told they aren't as spiritual as those who say they have seen God through angels. How do I convince them that Christ is enough?"

"I'll talk to them about some of those issues," Paul replies. "Maybe they'll listen to me." Read 2:6-23, asking God to speak to you about your life.

For Thought and Discussion: Read Ephesians 4:11-16. How do these verses help you to understand better how to be "rooted and built up in him"? What are the responsibilities of individuals to themselves? To the rest of the body?

Freedom in Christ (2:6-15)

1. The Colossians are encouraged to continue their lives in Christ (see 2:6). What do you think he meant when he told the Colossians they were to be "rooted and built up in him" (2:7)?

_____

_____

_____

_____

_____

_____

**Optional
Application:** As the
believers at Colosse
were taught what
to do, they were
"strengthened in the
faith" (2:7). Have you
established patterns
that put you in a
student's role, as one
who is being taught?
What might you do
to be strengthened
in the faith in this
manner?

2. How does a person or group go about being
rooted and built up in Christ, and strengthened
in the faith?

_____

_____

_____

_____

_____

_____

3. Why should we be "overflowing with thankfulness" (2:7)?

_____

_____

_____

_____

_____

Elemental spiritual forces of this world (2:8,20).
"This term . . . means false, worldly, religious,
elementary teachings. Paul was counteracting
the Colossian heresy, which, in part, taught
that for salvation one needed to combine faith
in Christ with secret knowledge and with man-
made regulations concerning such physical
and external practices as circumcision, eat-
ing and drinking, and observance of religious
festivals."[1]

Power and authority (2:10). Forces in the spiritual
world. Before knowing Christ, the Colossians
had paid homage to the gods of nature so that
their livelihoods would not be destroyed, to
the demons of night so that they would not
be harmed, and to the mistresses of fertility
so their futures would be guaranteed. Pagans
of Paul's day believed that hundreds of spiritual forces and beings dominated their lives.
Fear made astrology, magic, and religion—all

efforts to manage the spiritual forces—booming businesses.

4. Colossians 2:8 is in the form of a warning:
Watch out! The phrase "takes you captive" is
used in the sense of carrying someone away
from the truth into the slavery of error.[2] Why
do you think Paul thought it necessary to issue
such a strong warning?

_____

_____

_____

_____

Optional Application: Paul, scarred and in prison, can't seem to praise and thank God enough. Think of someone you know who always seems to be "overflowing with thankfulness." What kinds of hardships has that person been through? How do you think God would have you imitate his or her attitude?

Circumcision (2:11). In the Israelite faith, cutting
away the foreskin was the exclusive sign that a
man stood in covenant relation with God (see
Genesis 17:1-14).[3] Although other nations prac-
ticed circumcision, it was essential if a person
was to belong to Israel. The cutting represented
an oath that invoked a curse on oneself: it
invited God to cut off the man's life and heirs
if he broke his covenant with God.[4] Moses and
Jeremiah said that outward circumcision must
be accompanied by circumcision of one's heart
(see Deuteronomy 10:16; Jeremiah 4:4)—the
hard callous on the heart had to be cut away
just like a foreskin. Paul repeatedly faced Jewish
Christians who insisted that Gentile Christians
had to be physically circumcised in order to
become part of the new covenant with God.

Flesh (2:11,13). It is not just our bodies but the
human nature we are all born with, the nature
we inherit from sinful Adam and Eve. It is a
body with inclinations to do evil and a spirit
with rebellious tendencies toward God. The flesh
is the sum total of all that is evil in the person
who has not been changed by Christ. One who
is in this position is described as "in Adam." One
who has been renewed by Christ is described as
"in Christ," and the old nature has been "put
off."[5]

Baptism (2:12). When John the Baptist preached a "baptism of repentance for the forgiveness of sins" (Mark 1:4), he was talking about turning from sin to the coming Messiah. Later, Paul was able to teach that baptism also means identifying with Christ in His death and resurrection (see Romans 6:1-10). As Christ died and was buried, then rose again, so also the believer is buried in water (whether symbolically or literally) and raised again.

Just as circumcision is an outward and public sign of the old covenant, and burial is an outward and public sign that one has died, so baptism is an outward and public sign of faith in Christ.

5. Observe how the words "in Christ," "in him," "with him," and "by Christ" are used repeatedly throughout 2:9-12. What do you think is meant by each of these phrases?

"in Christ all the fullness of the Deity lives in bodily form"

_____

_____

_____

"you have been brought to fullness"

_____

_____

_____

"In him you were also circumcised"

_____

_____

60

_____

_____

_____

"circumcised by Christ"

_____

_____

_____

_____

_____

"having been buried with him in baptism"

_____

_____

_____

_____

_____

Optional Application: Thank God for what 2:9-15 says He has done for you. How should these gracious acts affect what you do?

Legal indebtedness (2:14). "A business term, meaning a certificate of indebtedness in the debtor's handwriting. Paul uses it as a designation for the Mosaic law, with all its regulations, under which everyone is a debtor to God."[6]

6. What has Christ's death and resurrection accomplished for you? In your own words, list everything you observe in 2:13-15.

_____

_____

_____

_____

_____

_____

7. How do you think these acts should affect the way you respond . . .

to Christ's forgiveness (compare 2:6-7; 3:1-3)?

_____

_____

_____

_____

_____

to rules and regulations others would like to impose on you (see 2:16-23)?

_____

_____

_____

_____

_____

Triumphing over them by the cross (2:15). Literally, "leading them in a triumphal procession." When a Roman general was victorious, he would bring captives back to Rome with him. He would enter the city at the head of a long procession of his soldiers and captives. The crowds would cheer and burn incense to celebrate this sign of total victory.[7]

8. When Jesus nailed the record of our debts to the cross, killing it by His own death, how did that make a public spectacle of the powers and authorities (wicked angels)?

_____

_____

_____

_____

Freedom from regulations (2:16-23)

"Therefore" (2:16) links this portion of the passage with what has gone before. All of our understanding of 2:16-23 — a list of "do nots" — ought to be founded on the previous list of what Christ has done, is doing, and will continue to do on behalf of His people.

By what you eat or drink (2:16). Because Jewish regulations did not include laws about beverages, this refers to more stringent rules of self-denial, including giving up meat and wine. Such rules became more than habits of good health when it was said that following them would help one have visions, gain enlightenment, or become more pleasing to God.[8]

Religious festival, a New Moon celebration or a Sabbath day (2:16). The Law of Moses commanded these for Jews, but they were not obligatory for Christians. Jesus fulfilled the meaning of those ceremonies and inaugurated a new covenant with new celebrations. Also, pagans in Colosse observed sacred days to honor the astrological calendar and the astral powers that supposedly influenced human affairs.[9] The false teachers may have been trying to impose on Christians a conglomeration of these two traditions.

False humility and the worship of angels (2:18). Like later Gnostics, the false teachers in Colosse may have taught that "God . . . was . . . so far above man that he could only be worshiped in the form of angels he had created."[10] This purported to be a humble attitude toward the supreme God, but it was a false humility. Those who worshiped angels as the mediators between God and humanity were really refusing to acknowledge Christ as the one mediator before whom they should bow.[11]

For Thought and Discussion: What should we do when we hear someone describing a vision he or she claims to have had?

9. The Jewish ceremonial laws were intended to symbolically depict the coming of Christ. Why don't Christians have to follow them (see 2:16-17)?

_____

_____

_____

_____

_____

10. a. What attitudes and actions does Paul condemn in 2:18?

_____

_____

_____

_____

_____

b. Does Paul mean that anyone who describes must be unspiritual and puffed up? Why or why not? (*Optional*: See 2 Corinthians 12:1-9; 1 John 4:1-3; Revelation 1:1-3,9-20.)

_____

_____

_____

_____

11. Why is it disastrous when part of the body of Christ loses connection with the Head by going off with its own notions (see 2:19)?

_____

_____

_____

_____

12. a. Why is submission to rules like "Do not handle! Do not taste! Do not touch!" an inferior
path to take (2:21)?

_____

_____

_____

_____

_____

b. How might following such regulations
deceive the believer (see 2:23)?

_____

_____

_____

_____

_____

c. Why can't such rules really restrain sensual
indulgence?

_____

_____

_____

_____

13. What was the most significant insight for you
from your study of Colossians 2:6-23?

_____

_____

_____

_____

**Optional
Application:**
a. How have you
been "held together"
(2:19) recently by your
relationship with
other parts of the
body of Christ? How
have you seen the
whole body of Christ,
perhaps in your
local assembly, hold
together under criti-
cism or even assault?
b. How can you
make sure you stay
connected to the
Head and supported
by the body's sinews?

For Thought and Discussion: Why do rules about abstaining from certain foods and drinks encourage false humility (see 2:23)?

For Further Study: Add 2:6-23 to your outline.

14. Based on what you have just studied, how do you think Christ would have you change a perception, an attitude, or an action to more completely follow Him this week?

_____

_____

_____

_____

_____

15. What steps can you take to do this?

_____

_____

_____

_____

16. Write down any questions you have about 2:6-23.

_____

_____

_____

_____

For the group

Worship.

Warm-up. To get to know each other a little better, ask each person to tell whether he or she sees himself or herself as a person who likes, tolerates, or dislikes rules. To a certain extent, the love of rules is a personality trait.

Read aloud and summarize.

Much ado about rules. Once you understand Paul's views on the rules being imposed on the Colossians, discuss one or both of the following sets of questions. Allow about fifteen minutes for each set.

(1) In what situations have the members of the group ever been where they felt rules were being imposed upon them? What was the nature of the rules? Were the rules legitimate and necessary, or unnecessary and harsh? What was the spirit with which the rules were enforced? How did they respond at the time? How have their perspectives changed in response to this situation?

(2) How do you think you ought to share your viewpoints without imposing rules? Are there any people with whom you need to exercise tolerance? Forgiveness? Thankfulness? What do you think God would have you begin to do this week?

1. Kenneth Barker, ed., *The NIV Study Bible* (Grand Rapids, MI: Zondervan, 1985), 1815.
2. Peter O'Brien, *Colossians, Philemon* (Waco, TX: Word, 1982), 109.
3. Barker, 1815.
4. Barker, 31.
5. Herbert M. Carson, *The Epistles of Paul to the Colossians and Philemon* (London: Tyndale, 1960), 66–67.
6. Barker, 1815.
7. Barker, 1765, 1815.
8. F. F. Bruce, *The Epistles to the Colossians, to Philemon, and to the Ephesians* (Grand Rapids, MI: Eerdmans, 1984), 114.
9. O'Brien, 139.
10. Barker, 1815–1816.
11. Carson, 74.

COLOSSIANS 3:1-11

Be Who You Are!

"Since, then" (3:1) tells us that Paul is about to draw conclusions from what he has been saying. Christ is supreme; He has freed us from the dominion of darkness; He has canceled the written code and disarmed the evil powers; He has released us from their delusive and oppressive rules. We have died with Christ and been raised with Christ. What then? Are we free to do whatever we want? Paul explains. Ask God to convict you as you read 3:1-11.

Keep looking up (3:1-4)

In his usual manner, Paul spends a lot of time laying the foundation for further truths. As an experienced evangelist and pastor, he knew that new concepts needed to be repeated and old ones reinforced. Now, he says, the foundation is laid; the Colossians know where they stand with God. They are ready to think about how to live in light of what they have just heard.

Seated at the right hand (3:1). The position of honor beside a king.[1] Psalm 45:9 portrays a king with his royal bride at his right hand; Psalm 110:1 describes God making a footstool out of the enemies of the person at His right hand.

Glory (3:4). The bliss of heaven.[2] In this context; the bliss of heaven includes receiving a

69

For Further Study:
Romans 6:1-11 points
out the relationship
between life and
death. How does
this passage help
you to see what Paul
is talking about in
Colossians 2:11-13 and
3:1?

resurrection body, just as Christ received one
upon His resurrection.[3]

1. "Since, then" not only connects this verse (3:1)
   with what was previously said; it also sets the
   stage to compare how different the believer's
   life is from his old life. Find at least four ways in
   3:1-4 that things have changed.

   a. _____

   _____

   _____

   b. _____

   _____

   _____

   c. _____

   _____

   _____

   d. _____

   _____

   _____

2. How do you think a person sets his or her heart
   and mind on "things above" (3:1-2)? (*Optional*:
   See Philippians 4:8-9.)

   _____

   _____

   _____

   _____

3. If you have been identified with Christ in His
   death and resurrection (see 3:1) and Christ is
   seated at the right hand of God, what does that
   say about your own relationship with God?

   _____

_____

_____

_____

_____

For Further Study:
In Philippians 3:19, Paul paints a picture of those who set their minds on "earthly things." What are the characteristics of such a person?

Study Skill — Cross-References

Passages of Scripture that help to explain a passage under consideration are called *cross-references*. Cross-references in the margin of your Bible or in a concordance can be used to explore concepts, such as "appear[ing] with him in glory" (3:4), or specific words, such as "glory." The rule of thumb is that the Bible is its own best interpreter, so if you can explain the Bible with the Bible, do it.

---

4. Although our lives are now hidden in Christ at the second coming of Jesus, everything will be brought into plain view. How do the following cross-references explain . . .

a. how the Christian's life is "hidden with Christ in God" (3:3)?

Romans 8:38-39 _____

_____

_____

Galatians 2:20 _____

_____

_____

(*Optional*: 1 Peter 1:3-6) _____

_____

_____

(*Optional*: Psalm 91:1-4) _____

_____

_____

71

b. what will happen when believers "appear with him in glory" (3:4)?

1 Corinthians 4:5 _____

_____

_____

1 John 3:2 _____

_____

_____

(*Optional*: Philippians 3:21)_____

_____

_____

Get rid of it (3:5-11)

Now that you are new men and women in Christ says Paul, act that way (see 3:5). Act and speak and think to make plain that you are no longer under the control of sin. Be who you are![4]

Put to death (3:5). Act as if the practices and attitudes of the old way of life are dead.[5] Work out in life experiences what has already happened internally.[6] The power that energized those old habits is slain, but it remains to uproot the habits themselves.

Sexual immorality (3:5). Includes prostitution, adultery, unchastity, fornication—every kind of unlawful sexual intercourse.[7] Because of the widespread traffic with prostitutes, some of Paul's churches had difficulty abandoning their former pagan tolerance of it.[8]

Impurity (3:5). The misuse of sex, especially immoral sexual conduct.[9] The word also applies to other forms of moral evil. For example, 1 Thessalonians 2:3 talks about "impure motives," denoting a general lack of integrity.[10]

72

Lust (3:5). Shameful passion that leads to sexual excesses.[11] In 1 Thessalonians 4:4-7, "passionate lust" wrongs the spouse of the one with whom the sexual immorality is done by taking that which belonged to the spouse. Lust may also be any sinful longing that leads away from God.[12]

Evil desires (3:5). "Desire" and "longing" were often used positively to express strong emotions, like Paul's longing to be with Christ (Philippians 1:23).[13] "Evil desires," then, are wicked longings, as in the case of one who looks lustfully at an individual, desiring to possess sexually him or her (see Matthew 5:28).

Greed, which is idolatry (3:5). A greedy person tries to gain satisfaction in something that does not lawfully belong to him or her. Because greed focuses on someone or something other than God, it is idolatrous.[14]

Wrath of God (3:6). God's anger at sin is expressed in judgment and punishment. The God of love and mercy is also a God of moral purity. He hates sin so much that He sent His Son to free us from it (see 2:9-15), and He intends to eradicate it utterly.

For Thought and Discussion: Does Paul think sexual immorality is worse than anger? Why or why not?

For Thought and Discussion: What is slander? Have you ever been slandered by a Christian? Are you still angry about it, or have you forgiven? Have you ever slandered someone else?

5. How do you think the vices listed in 3:5 are related to one another?

_____

_____

_____

_____

_____

6. Why do you think Paul found it necessary to urge the Colossians to rid themselves of such things as anger and slander (see 3:8) when they were already new creatures?

_____

_____

73

For Further Study:
Read Psalm 1:1 and
James 1:13-15. How
do these verses shed
light on the relation-
ship between the sins
listed in Colossians
3:5? Do such relation-
ships between con-
ception and birth of
sin always occur? Why
or why not?

**Optional
Application:**
When you were last
tempted to sin, did
you act as if that sin
had no power over
you? What happened
next?

**Optional
Application:** What
steps can you take
to put to death and
be rid of the vice you
named in question 7?

7. Which of the vices in 3:5,8-9 are you most
tempted to commit? Describe specifically what
this vice means in your life.

Taken off . . . put on . . . clothe yourselves
(3:9-10,12). The imagery is of taking off old,
filthy clothes and putting on new, clean ones.

8. How is taking off the old self and putting on the
new self like changing clothes (see 3:9-12)?

9. Do you think taking off and putting on sometimes requires great effort, or is it a simple task?
Why?

74

10. Is this merely an outward change, like changing clothes, or an inward one? Why is this important? (*Optional*: See Romans 12:2; Matthew 15:18-20.)

_____

_____

_____

_____

11. Is taking off and putting on a one-time action or a process? Explain (see Colossians 3:10; 2 Corinthians 3:18; 4:16; 5:17).

_____

_____

_____

_____

Gentile or Jew, circumcised or uncircumcised (3:11). This was a major division within the early church. Jews were raised to abhor many Gentile foods, customs, and beliefs. Many Jewish Christians had a hard time accepting the idea that Gentiles did not have to be circumcised or keep Jewish ceremonial laws in order to be Christians. For their part, Greeks thought their culture was superior to Jewish culture, objected to Jewish laws, and found circumcision disgusting.

Barbarian, Scythian (3:11). Originally, a barbarian was someone who did not speak Greek, so his speech sounded like "bar-bar" to Greeks. But the Greeks thought anyone who could not speak Greek was uncivilized. Scythians had a reputation for brutality; they were considered by others as little better than wild beasts. Scythians came from what is today south Russia.[15]

For Further Study:
Add 3:1-11 to your
outline.

Both Jews and Greeks were raised to be
unabashedly racist. Jews were taught to think
all non-Jews morally debased, and Greeks were
trained to consider all non-Greeks uncivilized
barbarians.

Slave or free (3:11). The class system in the Roman
Empire was as rigid a social barrier as race.
In several legal areas (religion was not one of
them), Roman law treated slaves as subhuman.

12. The Colossian church might well have included
Greeks, Jews, and barbarians, both slaves and
free persons. In such a church, why might the
exhortations to be rid of anger, slander, and so
on (see 3:8) have been especially appropriate?

_____

_____

_____

_____

_____

13. What sorts of diversity in your church, fellowship, or workplace make these exhortations
necessary for you?

_____

_____

_____

_____

_____

14. Summarize in one or two sentences your most
significant discoveries from Colossians 3:1-11.

_____

_____

_____

_____

_____

_____

_____

15. How have you seen any of the truths of 3:1-11 already at work in your life?

    _____

    _____

    _____

    _____

    _____

16. What action would you like to take this week to respond to something in this passage? (Questions 7 and 13 suggest some possibilities.)

    _____

    _____

    _____

    _____

    _____

17. List any questions you have about 3:1-11.

_____

_____

_____

_____

For the group

Worship.

Read aloud.

Summarize.

Questions. This lesson focuses on putting off and putting on. Once you think you understand the concept, take most of your time to apply Paul's exhortations to yourselves. Face up to questions 7 and 13, and discuss what you each can do. Be honest with each other about the failings you perceive in yourselves. If you find yourselves reluctant to share openly, recognize that you need to take steps to foster trust in your group. What are the obstacles to trust, and how can you overcome them? For example, are you afraid someone will gossip, lose respect for you, misunderstand, or be shocked by the real you?

Worship and prayer. You may wish to close the study session by pairing off to pray. Group members may prefer to share their problem areas regarding the sins in 3:5-9 with just one other person rather than with the whole group. Everyone must agree to be careful to preserve the privacy of others by not mentioning names or contexts ("someone in this group," "a woman at work").
　　Whether you pair off or remain together, take time to confess your areas of weakness. Then pray for each other that God will give you grace to put off those aspects of the old, dead nature and put on Christ's nature. Thank God for making this possible through Christ's death and resurrection.

To prepare. By now the group leader should have read the "For the group" section from the next lesson. This is the time to anticipate what is to come. For the discussion on psalms, hymns, and songs from the Spirit, you can assign one category to each of three members or teams of members. Each team will bring a psalm, hymn, or spiritual song for discussion and singing, using the questions listed. Group members may wish to bring a recording of a performance of the song, particularly if they are not musically inclined. The group leader also may arrange to have available copies of a church hymnal or psalter for group singing. A guitar or recorder or other instruments may be in order, as well. Be sure to read "Psalms, Hymns, and Songs from the Spirit" on pages 90–91 before choosing the song.

Differences in Kind

"By *members* [in 3:15] Paul meant what we should call *organs*, things essentially different from, and complementary to, one another: things differing not only in structure and function but also in dignity . . . I am afraid that when we describe a man as 'a member of the Church' we usually mean nothing Pauline: we mean only that he is a unit — that he is one more specimen of the same kind of thing as X and Y and Z. How true membership in a body differs from inclusion in a collective may be seen in the structure of a family. The grandfather, the parents, the grownup son, the child, the dog, and the cat . . . are not interchangeable. Each person is almost a species in himself. The mother is not simply a different person from the daughter, she is a different kind of person. The grown-up brother is not simply one unit in the class children, he is a separate estate of the realm. The father and grandfather are almost as different as the cat and the dog. If you subtract any one member you have not simply reduced the family in number, you have inflicted an injury on its structure. Its unity is a unity of unlikes.[16]

---

1. Kenneth Barker, ed., *The NIV Study Bible* (Grand Rapids, MI: Zondervan, 1985), 906.
2. M. G. Easton, *Illustrated Bible Dictionary* (Grand Rapids, MI: Baker, 1978), 299.
3. Barker, 1589, note on Luke 24:36.

4. F. F. Bruce, *The Epistles to the Colossians, to Philemon, and to the Ephesians* (Grand Rapids, MI: Eerdmans, 1984), 140–142.
5. Bruce, 141.
6. Herbert M. Carson, *The Epistles of Paul to the Colossians and Philemon* (London: Tyndale, 1960), 81.
7. Peter O'Brien, *Colossians, Philemon* (Waco, TX: Word, 1982), 181.
8. Bruce, 143.
9. O'Brien, 181.
10. Bruce, 143.
11. O'Brien, 182.
12. Easton, 441.
13. O'Brien, 182.
14. Carson, 82.
15. Barker, 1816.
16. C. S. Lewis, "Membership," *Fern Seed and Elephants* (London: Fount, 1975).

COLOSSIANS 3:12-17

Dressed in Holy Clothes

From 3:5-11 we have a pretty good idea of the old, dirty clothes we need to shed. But what are the new, beautiful garments we should wear instead? Reread 3:1-4, then read 3:12-17. Ask God to make these virtues a part of you as you study them.

New clothes (3:12-14)

God's chosen people (3:12). Just as Israel was called this (see Deuteronomy 4:37), so the Christian community is chosen as "a royal priesthood, a holy nation, God's special possession" (1 Peter 2:9). God's purpose was to create a people who, by their very being, would praise Him (see Ephesians 1:12; 1 Peter 2:9).

Compassion (3:12). Heartfelt sympathy that is shown in outward deeds of goodness.[1]

Kindness (3:12). Also "goodness," "generosity," "bounty," "courtesy." The word expresses the abundant bounty God displays to His people, as in a harvest that is not just adequate, but is overflowing.

Humility (3:12). The Old Testament says repeatedly that God will punish the proud and arrogant, and will exalt the lowly and humble (see Isaiah 2:6-22; Amos 2:6-7). The former think they have the resources to manage life on their own, and that they have great value independent of God.

81

For Thought and Discussion: How are the themes of being "chosen" and "dearly loved" (3:12) expanded in the following Scripture passages: Matthew 3:17; 12:15-21; 1 Thessalonians 1:4-5; 2 Thessalonians 2:13-17?

By contrast, the latter know they are nothing great apart from God, but are of great worth because they are made in God's image and are loved by Him. They also know they have no hope of survival without God.

Gentleness (3:12). Also "meekness." This is a near-synonym for humility, the two words are often paired in both Old and New Testaments.

The meek in the Old Testament were the poor people who did not own land. They were the defenseless, those without rights, who were oppressed, cheated, and exploited. In deep need, they sought help from God alone (see Psalm 40:17).[2]

The meek (humble, gentle) person does not have a low opinion of himself; he "is not occupied with self at all."[3] Because he trusts God's goodness and His control over situations, the meek person does not have to worry about self-interest, "looking out for Number One," or enhancing his status. To be meek or humble is to accept what God commands and ordains, and to seek help from God rather than trusting in one's own abilities. It is not a passive tolerance of injustice (especially toward others), but a reliance on God for vindication and a refusal to retaliate when insulted. The meek person is convinced that God's ways are good, so he neither disputes nor resists what God sends.

Jesus' meekness (see Matthew 11:29) did not conflict with His courage, concern for justice, and confidence that through the Father He was competent to do His job.

Patience (3:12). Longsuffering endures wrong and puts up with the exasperating conduct of others rather than flying into a rage or wanting revenge.[4]

1. Paul lists five virtues in 3:12. In each of the following cross-references, discover models for the clothing God wants His people to wear.

   Matthew 9:35-38 (compassion) _____

   _____

_____

_____

_____

_____

Luke 6:35 (kindness, goodness) _____

For Further Study:
a. For more examples of compassion, see Matthew 14:14; 15:32.
b. For more on goodness, see Psalm 25:6-10.

_____

_____

_____

_____

Philippians 2:6-11 (humility)_____

_____

_____

_____

_____

1 Peter 2:23 (gentleness, meekness) _____

_____

_____

_____

_____

Isaiah 48:9 (patience)_____

_____

_____

_____

_____

2. What does "bear with each other" mean (3:13)?

_____

_____

For Further Study:
Use a concordance
to find all the New
Testament references
to how Christians
should treat "one
another" or "each
other." Start with "do
not lie to each other"
(Colossians 3:9), "bear
with each other"
(Colossians 3:13), and
"love one another"
(John 13:34-35).

**Optional
Application:** Paul
says, "Forgive one
another if any of
you has a grievance"
(3:13). Nothing should
be left unforgiven.
Are there grievances
that you have not for-
given your brother or
sister in Christ? What
do you think you
ought to do about it?

3. How do 1:21-22 and 2:13-14 help you understand what it means to "forgive as the Lord for-
gave you" (3:13)? (*Optional*: Compare Ephesians
2:1-7.)

_____

_____

_____

_____

_____

4. How does getting involved with other
Christians in a church or fellowship help us
develop compassion, gentleness, patience, for-
bearance, forgiveness, and so on?

_____

_____

_____

_____

5. "On top of all the other 'articles of clothing,'"
we must put on love.[5] How does love bind all
the other Christian graces together (see 3:14)?

_____

_____

_____

_____

6. We should practice all these virtues among non-believers as well, but why is it especially crucial that we practice them among "one another"? (See John 13:35; 17:23; 1 Corinthians 12:12-26; Colossians 3:11-12,15.)

_____

_____

_____

_____

_____

For Thought and Discussion: Read Luke 11:2-4. What relationships do you see in these verses and in Colossians 3:13 between God's forgiveness and our forgiveness of others?

Optional Application: What are the playing fields in your life where Christ is to umpire (see 3:15)?

Let Christ work (3:15-17)

Rule (3:15). Umpire, referee, arbitrate, moderate.

7. Think of all the problems an umpire prevents and of the contributions he or she makes. How do you think the "peace of Christ" (3:15) functions like an umpire?

_____

_____

_____

_____

_____

8. The "message of Christ" came to the Colossians mostly in oral form, though it included the written Old Testament, as well.[6] Several actions are required in 3:16. How do you think each of the following actions are to be fulfilled? (Use the context of the phrase and your own understanding and experience.)

"Let the message of Christ dwell among you richly"

_____

_____

For Thought and Discussion: In the middle of this discussion of peace, love, and other virtues, Paul says simply, "And be thankful" (3:15). What do you think Paul is telling the Colossians to be thankful for? How do you think ungratefulness affects peace in your faith community?

"teach and admonish one another" _____

_____

_____

_____

_____

"through psalms, hymns, and songs from the Spirit"

_____

_____

_____

_____

Study Skill — The Way It Was

What does Paul mean by singing "psalms, hymns, and songs from the Spirit"? And why does he think this is so important? To answer that and other questions that begin with "Why," we need to discover the way it was for Paul. In this case, what was Paul's religious background? How might Paul in his worship practices have been imitating Jesus? How was worship together important for the Jewish community? What was the place of the synagogue in Jewish life? What did the Christians carry over from synagogue worship to Christian services? Answers to these questions may be found by using a Bible dictionary or other reference book. Look for related words: "synagogue," "worship," and "Sabbath." The box on pages 42–44, "Praise to Christ, the First, the Best" is a start, and the box on pages 90–91, "Psalms, Hymns, and Songs from the Spirit" adds more.

Next time you're puzzled by a "why" question read up on a little history.

9. Verse 17 moves out of the context of worship to include all of life—everything. A list of vices and virtues helps, but it doesn't provide every guideline for speech and conduct. What does Paul say should be included in every deed? What is meant by each guideline?

For Further Study: Add 3:12-17 to your outline.

a. _____

_____

_____

this means: _____

_____

_____

_____

b. _____

_____

_____

_____

this means: _____

_____

_____

_____

10. What insights from this study about how Christians ought to behave did you find most helpful?

_____

_____

_____

_____

_____

_____

11. What growth in the areas Paul describes have you seen in yourself over the last year or so?

_____

_____

_____

_____

_____

12. What aspect of these instructions do you find most difficult?

_____

_____

_____

_____

13. What action can you take to put into practice something in 3:12-17, especially in the area you just named? (Ask God what you should concentrate on.)

_____

_____

_____

_____

14. Write down any questions you have about 3:12-17.

_____

_____

_____

_____

For the group

Worship. Sing some songs of praise and thanks—some psalms set to music or a Christian song.

Read aloud.

Summarize.

The virtues. On a chalkboard or easel, make a list of the vices Paul names in 3:5-10. Next to it, make a list of the virtues he gives in 3:12-14. After you've discussed the meaning and importance of each virtue (questions 1 through 6), take a few minutes to let everyone share how his or her efforts to put to death the vices have been going. What have you learned about yourselves? (It is not uncommon to perceive oneself as getting worse when one begins to concentrate on a particular area.) Then ask, "How would acquiring these virtues help us put off those vices?"

Next, let group members share what growth they have seen in themselves regarding the virtues, and which one area they most want to grow in. Then, if you feel you know each other well enough, encourage one another by pointing out the ways you have seen each other show compassion, kindness, and so on. Or, describe how you have seen someone else in your church or fellowship practice one of these virtues. Finally, plan together some action you can each take to exercise or develop one of these virtues. Commit yourselves to praying for each other about this.

Psalms, hymns, and songs from the Spirit. After discussing questions 7 through 9, let each team share its song. Each team should answer the following questions:

1. Is this a psalm, a hymn, or a song from the Spirit? Why do you think so?
2. What Scripture passage or doctrine is the song based on?
3. What are the song's major themes?
4. Who wrote the words and music? What do you know about him, her, or them?
5. What does the song mean to you? Why do you like it?

As each presentation is made, the group may add to the discussion. Then sing, perform, or play the music once through. If time is short, the group may choose to save one or two presentations for the next one or two sessions.

Psalms, Hymns, and Songs from the Spirit

"Singing is the most genuinely popular element in Christian worship," says Geoffrey Wainwright. "Familiar words and music, whether it be repeated response to biddings in a litany or the well-known phrases of a hymn, unite the whole assembly in active participation to a degree which is hardly true of any other component in the liturgy."[7] No wonder we are told to sing "psalms, hymns, and songs from the Spirit" (Colossians 3:16). But what is a psalm, and how is it different from a hymn or song from the Spirit?

"Psalms" refers to the Old Testament psalms (Luke 20:42, for example), some of which may have been set to music by the church. "Psalm" could also describe a song newly composed for Christian worship, such as the "hymn" in 1 Corinthians 14:26, where the translation is literally "psalm."[8]

A hymn is described by Augustine as "a song with praise to God."[9] Let's look at the three elements of his description: (1) "Praise" is a declaration and exaltation of someone's (in this case, God's) deeds and attributes. (2) "A song" means the hymn is not just a piece of poetry, but is intended to be sung. Furthermore, says hymnologist Eric Routley, a hymn is intended to be sung together.[10] (3) A hymn ought to be directed to God, whether by formally addressing Him ("We Worship Thee, O God") or more indirectly ("O God, Our Help in Ages Past).[11] Some of our most important Christian doctrines are expressed in hymns preserved for us now only in Paul's letters (see Colossians 1:15-20; Ephesians 5:14; Philippians 2:6-11; 1 Timothy 3:16).[12]

"Songs from the Spirit" recount the acts of God and praise Him for them.[13] "Worthy is the Lamb," for example (see Revelation 5:9-12), recounts the sacrifice of the Lamb of God and sings that He is worthy "to receive power and

wealth and wisdom and strength and honor and glory and praise!" The term may mean "songs inspired by the Spirit" — songs that were the result of immediate inspiration, as in the scene in 1 Corinthians 14:26 where improvised compositions are brought to the assembly and used in worship.[14]
The point seems to be: Sing! Together!

1. H. Dermot McDonald, *Commentary on Colossians and Philemon* (Waco, TX: Word, 1982), 114.
2. Peter O'Brien, *Colossians, Philemon* (Waco, TX: Word, 1982), 200.
3. W. E. Vine, "Meek," *An Expository Dictionary of New Testament Words* (Nashville: Royal Publishers, 1952), 728. See also Wolfgang Bauder, "Humility, Meekness," *The New International Dictionary of New Testament Theology*, ed. Colin Brown, vol. 2 (Grand Rapids, MI: Zondervan, 1976), 256–259.
4. O'Brien, 201.
5. O'Brien, 203.
6. Kenneth Barker, ed., *The NIV Study Bible* (Grand Rapids, MI: Zondervan, 1985), 1817.
7. Ralph P. Martin, *The Worship of God* (Grand Rapids, MI: Eerdmans, 1982), 42, in Geoffrey Wainwright, *Doxology: The Praise of God in Worship, Doctrine, and Life* (New York: Oxford University Press, 1980), 200.
8. Kenneth Barker, 1817. Rich collections of psalms have been available to the church for hundreds of years, such as *The Scottish Psalter*, which goes back to 1650 and is still in use among Scottish Presbyterians. *The Book of Psalms for Singing* (Pittsburgh, PA: Board of Education and Publication, Reformed Presbyterian Church of North America, 1973) draws largely from *The Scottish Psalter*. The Episcopal Church provides a translation in the *Book of Common Prayer* (New York: The Church Hymnal Corporation, 1979) that can be sung or chanted using service music from their *Hymnal 1982* (New York: The Church Hymnal Corporation, 1985). Psalm-singing has been made easy with the *Psalter Hymnal*, published by the Christian Reformed Church (Grand Rapids, MI: Board of Publications of the Christian Reformed Church, 1976).
9. Martin, 42.
10. Martin, 42, in Wainwright, 47. From Eric Routley, *Hymns for Church and School* (London: Novello, 1964), iv.
11. Martin, 42, in Wainwright, 43–44.
12. Barker, 1817.

91

13. Barker, 1817.
14. Martin, 42, in Wainwright, 53. The folk music wave of the 1960s gave birth to many such songs from the Spirit, accompanied by that old instrument of improvisation, the guitar. Several collections are now available from music publishers at your local Christian bookstore. Among the best are those that add music to Scripture, such as the *Scripture in Song* series (Costa Mesa, CA: Scripture in Song Publishing, 1979) and *Scripture Praise* (Waco, TX: Lexicon Music, 1978).

COLOSSIANS 3:18–4:1

How to Live at Home

Now Paul provides guidelines for the most familiar relationships—those between members of a household. A traveling evangelist like Paul was probably better acquainted with how Christian households were managed than almost anyone else. Church members might have shared with Paul things they didn't tell their own pastor; certainly, he would have discerned patterns of behavior as he stayed in different homes on his journeys. From this perspective, Paul creates a framework of principles for how a Christian home should be built. He divides the principles he presents into three pairs: wives and husbands, children and parents, and slaves and masters. Read 3:18–4:1, and prayerfully examine the roles you may fill in each of these pairs.

Wives and husbands (3:18-19)

Submit (3:18). One of the results associated with the filling of the Holy Spirit (see Ephesians 5:18-21). "To submit meant to yield one's own rights. If the relationship called for it, as in the military, the term could connote obedience, but that meaning is not called for here. In fact, the word 'obey' does not appear in Scripture with respect to wives, though it does with respect to children . . . and slaves. . . ."[1]

93

Paul says a wife should submit to her husband because "the husband is the head of the wife as Christ is the head of the church" (Ephesians 5:22-23). From the meaning of "head", what do you think this says about how a wife submits to her husband?

Study Skill — Parallel Passages

When two or more passages of Scripture are nearly identical or deal with the same event, they are said to be "parallel." By putting the passages side by side, you can see Scripture reinforced, note how ideas are explained more fully in one passage, and follow themes through the Bible.

Passages in the New Testament that parallel passages in the Old Testament may demonstrate how prophecy was fulfilled by Jesus, for example (see Isaiah 61:1-2; Luke 4:17-21). In the Gospels, parallel passages provide a different point of view on similar teaching (see Matthew 5:1-12; Luke 6:17-23). And Paul often would treat a subject more fully in one passage than its parallel (see Ephesians 5:22–6:9; Colossians 3:18–4:1).

---

1. Colossians 3:18-21 is paralleled in Ephesians 5:22–6:4. The Ephesians passage is preceded by the command, "Submit to one another out of reverence for Christ" (5:21). How do you think this requirement sets the pattern for the relationship between wife and husband?

   _____

   _____

   _____

   _____

   _____

2. Submission is a vague concept until we get down to real situations. Imagine that you are a wife. What do you think would be submission that is "fitting in the Lord" (3:18) in the following circumstances (choose three):

   a. Your husband wants to move to enhance his career; you want to stay where you are for your career.

   _____

   _____

_____

_____

_____

b. Your husband wants you to lie to his boss for
him.

_____

_____

_____

_____

**For Thought and
Discussion:** Why is it
"fitting in the Lord"
to submit to one's
husband (3:18)? See
Ephesians 5:22-24. Are
there any acts of sub-
mission that would
not be fitting in the
Lord? If so, what are
some of them? If not,
why not?

c. Your husband wants to buy a particular
new car; you think you can't afford such an
expensive car.

_____

_____

_____

_____

_____

d. Your husband refuses to help with the house-
work even though you both have full-time
paying jobs.

_____

_____

_____

_____

e. You want to spend time in church activities;
your husband objects.

_____

_____

Optional Application: If you are married, think of how you treat your spouse. How do you speak of your spouse to other people? What specific ways do you think God would have you be a more loving, submissive spouse?

_____

_____

_____

3. What specific responsibilities of a husband to his wife do you find in the following verses?

Colossians 3:19 _____

_____

_____

Ephesians 5:25-33 _____

_____

_____

_____

_____

4. Imagine that you are a husband. What do you think Christlike love would be in the following circumstances (choose three):

a. You want to move to enhance your career; your wife wants to stay where you are.

_____

_____

_____

_____

_____

_____

b. Your job demands overtime if you are to move ahead; your wife wants you to spend more time with her and your children.

_____

_____

_____

_____

_____

c. You want to come home from work and be
   alone for awhile; your wife wants to talk with
   you when you get home.

_____

_____

_____

_____

_____

d. Your wife wants a new car; you think you
   can't afford one.

_____

_____

_____

_____

_____

e. You want to spend more time in church activities; your wife objects.

_____

_____

_____

_____

_____

5. How do the following Scriptures draw wife and
   husband together?

   1 Corinthians 11:11-12 _____

_____

**For Thought and
Discussion:**
   a. What happens
in a marriage when
either partner does
not follow the com-
mands of Colossians
3:18-19?
   b. What do you
think a wife should
do in response to
her husband's harsh-
ness or other symp-
toms of lack of love?
What do you think a
husband should do
in response to his
wife's disrespect or
other symptoms of
unsubmissiveness?
   c. How is Christ
the perfect example
of how each partner
ought to respond?

97

For Thought
and Discussion:
Ephesians 6:2 reminds
children that they are
also to "honor [their]
father and mother."
What do you think
are the similarities
between honor and
obedience? What are
the differences?

For Thought and
Discussion: Why do
you think Paul singles
out fathers as the
ones who are not
to discourage their
children?

Ephesians 5:31-33 _____

Children and parents (3:20-21)

Obey (3:20). Unlike "submit" in 3:18, which suggests *voluntary* submission, the word "obey" denotes absolute obedience.[2]

In everything (3:20,22). A Christian family is the context for the command to children, where parental orders are not contrary to the law of Christ.[3] The same phrase in regard to slaves also means "in everything not sinful" (see Acts 5:29).[4]

6. What factors are to motivate a child's obedience to his or her parents (see Colossians 3:20; Ephesians 6:1-3)?

7. Paul explains that if fathers embitter their children, the children will lose heart and come to think that it is useless trying to please their parents[5] (see Colossians 3:21; Ephesians 6:4). What do you think these verses indicate about the father's significance in the home?

_____

_____

_____

_____

8. How can parents, especially fathers, avoid embittering their children? What concrete actions and attitudes should they practice and avoid?

_____

_____

_____

_____

_____

_____

_____

Slaves and masters (3:22–4:1)

When Paul starts talking about wives, children, and slaves — hot social issues in that day — it is helpful to know something about the social context he was dealing with. See "The Roman Household" on pages 102–103.

9. What attitudes are slaves to have toward their work (see 3:22-25)? List at least three characteristics of a godly slave.

_____

_____

_____

_____

_____

_____

For Thought and Discussion: Can you think of ways that you have embittered your children or have seen this occur between other parents and children? What do you think should have been done differently?

For Thought and Discussion: What do you think happens when the children of Christian parents become bitter and discouraged? Why might this be a particularly difficult situation for both the children and their parents?

10. Why would it have been encouraging to slaves to know that they would someday receive an inheritance from the Lord as a reward, because He was the one they were serving (see 3:24)?

_____

_____

_____

_____

_____

11. Paul exhorts masters to provide their slaves with what is "right and fair" (4:1). In his world, "right and fair" for a slave would have meant reasonable work hours, good food, adequate shelter, and the opportunity for slaves to earn their freedom. Whether you are a supervisor or a manager of a household, there are people who answer to you. How do you think you are to be "right and fair" to those who are responsible to you?

_____

_____

_____

_____

_____

12. The ultimate motivation for both slave and master (see 3:23; 4:1) is that they serve one Master, the Lord. How should this affect the way you serve those over you or oversee those under you? Be as specific as possible.

3:23 _____

_____

_____

_____

4:1 _____

_____

_____

_____

13. What threads run through all of Paul's exhortations in 3:18–4:1?

_____

_____

_____

_____

_____

14. Which one instruction would you like to concentrate on for application?

_____

_____

_____

_____

15. How can you do this?

_____

_____

_____

_____

16. List any questions you have about 3:18–4:1.

_____

_____

_____

For Thought and Discussion:
a. Who do you think Paul is talking about in Colossians 3:25?

b. What difference might 3:25 have made in how slaves conducted themselves when their masters were cruel or unfair?

c. What difference do you think 3:25 should make in how you respond in a similar situation?

For Further Study:
a. How do Colossians 3:11 and 1 Timothy 6:1-2 broaden your understanding of how slave and master are to be related to one another?

b. How should these passages affect the way you relate to your boss and those you supervise?

For Further Study:
Add 3:18–4:1 to your outline.

For the group

Questions. Questions 2 and 4 could monopolize a lot of your time. You might want to choose just two situations from each question to discuss. Be prepared for disagreement. Also, keep an eye on the time so that you will have enough to share how you each plan to apply Paul's teaching.

Worship. If presentations on psalms, hymns, and songs from the Spirit are still waiting, the group may focus its worship time on the one or two that remain.

The Roman Household

The church at Colosse consisted mostly of Roman households. At the head or heart of the Roman household was the father, whose power was all-pervasive. He represented the family before the family gods (or God) and, as the oldest male ancestor, he had power over all his children and grandchildren until he specifically freed them to become heads of their own families.[6]

Such status was not necessarily negative. In an ideal situation, the father would give his child capital with which to trade and prosper. He would set him up in business or support him in a useful career. Mutual obligations would be fulfilled; the purpose was a natural and enriching relationship between two personalities.[7]

A patriarchal family did not have to be dictatorially organized. Roman sons, whose futures were dependent upon the interworkings of the family, held the privilege of participation in the family councils, where family matters were discussed and decided. Other members of the family were also allowed to act freely with a proportion of the family assets.[8]

The authority of the head of a household extended over his wife, as well. Legally, a Roman husband had more extensive power over his wife than did a Jewish husband; she was, in fact, in the same legal position as his children.[9] Her life was one of legal incapacity that amounted to enslavement, while her status was described as "imbecilitas," from which we get the word "imbecile."[10] Paul uses this relationship as a metaphor of the believer's (the wife's) release from the law (only if her husband dies) in Romans 7:1-4.

In Roman law, the authority and power exercised by the head of a household over his slaves was that of ownership. Although laws existed to maintain humane conditions, slave life still could be miserable and demanding. On the other hand, a good master would look after his slaves, even entrusting them with capital with which to trade. Although the profits technically belonged to the master, it was not unusual for the master to allow the slave to "keep" his profits and eventually "buy" his freedom.[11]

In his letters, Paul focuses, not on the legal rights endowed by Rome, but on the law of love inherited from Christ. Perhaps the Roman household was not to be restructured (though in some cases it had deteriorated so badly that complete rebuilding was necessary), but the way it operated was to change drastically under the mastery of Christ.

1. Kenneth Barker, ed., *The NIV Study Bible* (Grand Rapids, MI: Zondervan, 1985), 1798, notes on Ephesians 5:2.
2. Peter O'Brien, *Colossians, Philemon* (Waco, TX: Word, 1982), 224.
3. F. F. Bruce, *The Epistles to the Colossians, to Philemon, and to the Ephesians* (Grand Rapids, MI: Eerdmans, 1984), 165.
4. Barker, 1817.
5. Bruce, 165.
6. Francis Lyall, *Slaves, Citizens, Sons: Legal Metaphors in the Epistles* (Grand Rapids, MI: Zondervan, 1984), 120–121.
7. Lyall, 121.
8. Lyall, 122–125.
9. Lyall, 124.
10. John R. W. Stott, *God's New Society: The Message of Ephesians* (Downers Grove, IL: InterVarsity, 1979), 224.
11. Lyall, 124–125.

COLOSSIANS 4:2-18

And Finally

This last section illustrates the two faces of a biblical epistle: timeless instructions from the Spirit of God to all Christians (see 4:2-6); and personal comments from a very human writer to certain people on a specific occasion (see 4:7-18). But even the newsy bits of this personal letter are part of God's Word and give us insight into living the Christian life. Read 4:2-18, asking God to show you how these insights can be practically applied to your life.

Prayer and testimony (4:2-6)

Devote (4:2). "Persevere" (NEB) or "continue steadfastly" (RSV). The idea is that of a boat that always stands ready for someone to use or of an activity that one is devoted to or busily engaged in.[1]

Watchful (4:2). "With mind awake" (NEB), "keeping alert" (NASB).

Seasoned with salt (4:6). A favorite phrase because of its many applications. In this context it points to the use of salt to enhance the flavor of food and to preserve food from corruption.[2] In conversation, "wit" is the opposite of "insipidity"—the lack of flavor.[3] Be witty, but don't be obscene. (See also Ephesians 4:29, "unwholesome talk"; 5:4, "foolish talk"; Colossians 3:8, "filthy language.")

1. Why do you think Christians are to keep alert or watchful (see 4:2)? What should we be alert for? (*Optional*: See Luke 12:35-48; 1 Peter 5:8-9.)

_____

_____

_____

_____

2. In light of what you have already studied in Colossians, what reasons do believers have to be thankful in their prayers (see 4:2)?

_____

_____

_____

_____

_____

3. This is the sixth time Paul has mentioned thankfulness in this letter (see 1:3,12; 2:7; 3:15,17; 4:2). Why is thankfulness so important for Christians?

_____

_____

_____

_____

_____

4. a. What does Paul want the Colossians to pray for (see 4:3-4)?

_____

_____

_____

_____

_____

b. How is this like and unlike his prayer for them (see 1:9-12)?

_____

_____

_____

_____

_____

c. Why do you think the prayer of 4:3-4 is so important?

_____

_____

_____

_____

5. In the following examples of how Christians are to act wisely toward outsiders—unbelievers—what do you think Paul means?

"make the most of every opportunity" (4:5)

_____

_____

_____

_____

_____

"conversation . . . full of grace, seasoned with salt" (4:6)

_____

_____

_____

_____

_____

For Thought and Discussion:
a. A situation that is so unexpected that it seems intentionally unreasonable is said to be *ironic*. For instance, the fact that Jesus, the King of kings, was born in a cattle stall is ironic. Given Paul's circumstances, what do you find that is ironic about his request for open doors? For further understanding, read Acts 28:17-20,30-31 and Philippians 1:12-18.
b. What does this tell you about you and your circumstances?

Optional Application: Compare Colossians 4:5-6 to 1 Peter 3:15-16. How do your dealings with non-Christians reflect these principles? Look for opportunities to apply them this week. Ask God to help you.

Optional Application: What opportunities do you have to be with unbelievers? What do you think is your reputation among them? Why do you think it is important for you to maintain — or improve — your reputation for "conversation . . . full of grace, seasoned with salt"? What do you think God would have you do to be prepared better to "answer everyone"?

"know how to answer everyone" (4:6)

_____

_____

_____

_____

_____

Everyone says hello (4:7-18)

6. From 4:7-14, what do you discover about Paul's relationship with his associates?

_____

_____

_____

_____

_____

7. Aristarchus was a Macedonian Jew; Onesimus was a slave; Epaphras was a native Colossian pastor; Nympha was a Laodicean woman (see 4:9-15). What do these facts tell you about the effect of the gospel?

_____

_____

_____

_____

_____

_____

8. What message do you think was transmitted to outsiders by the relationships among the believers mentioned here?

_____

_____

_____

_____

_____

_____

9. What do you discover about the relationship between the churches in Colosse, Laodicea, and Hierapolis (see 4:13-16)?

_____

_____

_____

_____

_____

10. What was the most significant thing you learned from 4:2-18?

_____

_____

_____

_____

11. How is this truth relevant to your life? How would you like it to affect your life more than it already is?

_____

_____

For Further Study: The second chapter of Titus is a description of what must be taught to each group of people in the church — women, men, and slaves.
  a. Each time Paul finishes outlining what the group is to be taught, why does he say such teaching is necessary? How does this help you understand how Christians are to act wisely toward outsiders?
  b. What further light does Titus 2 shed on your study of Colossians 3:18–4:6?

Optional Application: How might the relationship between the churches in Asia be an example to your community of faith?

109

For Further Study:
Add 4:2-18 to your
outline.

_____

_____

_____

12. What steps can you take this week to begin
cooperating with God to bring this about?

_____

_____

_____

_____

13. Write down any questions you have about 4:2-18.

_____

_____

_____

_____

For the group

Warm-up. It's a good idea to check back with each
other to see how your applications are going. What
opportunities did you have to apply 3:18–4:1? What
happened when you tried? What did you learn?

Read aloud.

Summarize.

Questions.

Prayer. After you have completed the study questions, devote yourselves to prayer, following the
pattern Paul outlines in Colossians 1:3-14; 4:2-4.
You may apply Paul's instructions, remembering
Christians around the world who are imprisoned for
their faith. You may also wish to name the "outsiders" with whom you have contact and whom you
must "know how to answer."

Structure this prayer time as you wish. You can pray in pairs or all together; you can pray spontaneously or assign thanks, prayer for outsiders, prayer for those in prison, and so on, to different members. The leader should encourage the group to follow Paul's pattern by including all the elements, even if the order is not followed.

Worship. Complete the presentations on psalms, hymns, and songs from the Spirit, if you have not yet done so. If you have finished, sing a song or two before or after your study.

Beginner's Guide to Prayer

"In prayer, I also need to emphasize to you that much depends on strong resolution for beginners. There are many reasons for this, but I shall just mention a few.

"The first is that since God has given us so much, and since He still continues to bless us, it is proper that we should be resolved to be serious with Him, and so give Him our prayers from the heart. If we give time to others, does the Lord deserve less than they? Do not let us think that time is our own, but give to Him all of it entirely.

"The second reason for determination is that the devil has much less power to tempt us when we are in prayer. He is much afraid of resolute souls, for he knows from experience that these do him much mischief.

"A third reason is that a resolute soul fights with greater courage. It knows that, come what may, he must not turn back."[4]

---

1. Peter O'Brien, *Colossians, Philemon* (Waco, TX: Word, 1982), 237.
2. Allen C. Myers, ed., *The Eerdmans Bible Dictionary* (Grand Rapids, MI: Eerdmans, 1987), 904.
3. J. B. Lightfoot, *Saint Paul's Epistles to the Colossians and to Philemon* (London: Macmillan, 1875), 230–231.
4. Saint Teresa of Avila, *A Life of Prayer* (Portland, OR: Multnomah, 1983), 66.

REVIEW OF COLOSSIANS

After studying a book in detail for several weeks, it is often helpful to pull together what you have learned and examine the book as a whole again. A review can enable you to see how each individual topic the author talks about contributes to the overall point he wants to make. It can also help you trace themes and related ideas from chapter to chapter. This review is fairly thorough. Feel free to take extra time to complete it or to omit some sections.

1. Reread all of Colossians. It should be familiar to you by now, so you should be able to read rapidly, looking for threads that tie the book together. Pray for a fresh perspective on what God is saying through this book.

   Also, review lesson 1 of this study, as well as any outlines or charts you made of Colossians. You might also look at the end of each lesson in this study for summaries you made or significant truths you discovered. This may sound like a lot of work, but it will help you make connections among things you've learned and commit important truths to memory.

2. In lesson 1, question 4, you said tentatively what you thought the main theme or purpose of this letter was. After closer study, how would you now summarize Paul's apparent main goal?

   _____

   _____

_____

_____

_____

_____

3. Many students divide Colossians into four main
   sections between the introduction and the
   farewell. You may find that just summarizing
   these four sections will help you see the book as
   a whole. Write down a sentence or title that you
   think explains the point of each passage.

   1:1-14 **Thanksgiving and Prayers**_____

   _____

   1:15-23 _____

   _____

   _____

   _____

   1:24–2:5 _____

   _____

   _____

   _____

   _____

   2:6-23 _____

   _____

   _____

   _____

   _____

3:1–4:6 _____

_____
_____
_____
_____
_____

4:7-18 **_Everyone says hello_** _____

_____

4. What were the most important lessons you
learned from your study of Colossians on the
following topics?

thanksgiving and prayer _____

_____
_____
_____
_____

freedom in Christ_____

_____
_____
_____

how to live a holy life _____

_____
_____
_____
_____

how to live at home _____

_____

_____

_____

_____

_____

how to live in God's household _____

_____

_____

_____

_____

_____

other _____

_____

_____

_____

_____

5. One of the major topics of the letter is how Christ is superior. Summarize what Paul has to say about how Christ is supreme and all we need.

1:18-20 _____

_____

_____

_____

_____

_____

_____

2:2-3 _____

_____

_____

_____

_____

2:9-10 _____

_____

_____

_____

2:13-14 _____

_____

_____

_____

_____

6. In each of the following verses, Paul tells
   Christians to take off something and to put on
   something in its place. List how a believer's
   wardrobe is to change.

3:1-2 Take off	3:1-2 Put on
3:5-9 Take off	3:12 Put on

3:9 Take off	3:10 Put on
3:13 Take off	3:14 Put on

7. Have you noticed any areas (thoughts, attitudes, opinions, behavior) in which you have changed as a result of studying Colossians? If so, explain how you have changed.

_____

_____

_____

_____

_____

_____

8. Look back over the entire study at questions in which you expressed a desire to make some specific application. Are you satisfied with your follow-through? Pray about any of those areas that you think you should continue to pursue specifically. Write any notes here.

_____

_____

_____

_____

_____

_____

_____

9. Review the questions you listed at the ends of lessons 1 through 9. Do any important ones remain unanswered? If so, some of the sources in Study Aids may help you answer some of them. You might also study some particular passage again on your own, or ask a mature believer.

For the group

Read aloud. It might take fifteen minutes to read the whole letter to the Colossians aloud. You will probably find that this will refresh everyone's memory. However, if you prefer to save time, try reading just chapter 1.

Teaching. Unless you plan to take more than one meeting to cover this review, or unless your group is very adept at summarizing a book's teaching on a topic, you may want to select a few of the topics in questions 4 through 6 for discussion. Choose those that you think are most important for your group to grasp. Then ask several people to tell how they would summarize Paul's message (question 2).

Let everyone ask his or her unanswered questions. Instead of allowing the group to rely on the leader for answers, suggest that various group members pursue answers in books or other sources. It is wise to begin training members to take as much responsibility as possible in the group. However, the leader should give whatever guidance is needed.

Application. Give everyone a chance to share answers to questions 7 and 8. You should know each other well enough by now to be specific. Hopefully, you have been sharing progress on application periodically and have been helping each other plan and follow through on applications. You have probably also been praying for each other. So, this should not be a time of boasting or despair, but of humility and mutual encouragement.

PHILEMON
Historical Background

Paul wrote this short letter to Philemon probably at the same time as he wrote Colossians, AD 60–62. It was probably sent to Colosse, Philemon's home, along with the letter to the Colossians. Epaphras, planter of the Colossian church, and Onesimus, the slave in question, very likely carried the letters back with them. We deduce this from the names and circumstances mentioned in Colossians 4:7-17 and in Philemon.

The story so far

Along with other believers in Colosse, Philemon was a slave owner. One of his slaves, Onesimus, had apparently stolen from him (see Philemon 18), then run away. Under Roman law, this was punishable by death.[1]

Slavery

Slavery was an institution in the Roman Empire, with slaves constituting perhaps one-third of the population in Rome and other great cities.[2] Gaius who wrote a law book at the time of Paul, stated that there were basically two different kinds of people: free and slave.[3] Slaves had no legal personality—legally, they were property, not people. Their owners held absolute power over them.[4]

The only way a slave was different from other physical assets of the owner, such as cattle and property, was that he or she could become free.[5] Freedom was made possible by the *peculium*, a fund that the slave received from his owner and that he was free to use. Though in practice the slave might use this money to buy his freedom, legally, the *peculium* and the profits on investments made with it belonged to the master.[6] Regardless of the *peculium*, an owner would often free his slave after twenty years of work.[7]

Owners generally recognized that slaves worked better if their conditions were more like freedom. This perspective encouraged masters to allow the owning of property and the contracting of marriages.[8] Cruelty was condemned by a growing sentiment that slaves, as human beings, had at least as much right to life as animals did. By Philemon's time, this feeling had resulted in protective legislation that was more akin to our present laws protecting animal rights than human rights.[9]

Slavery in the United States was not so kind. In the mid-1600s, the Virginia House of Burgesses declared that African laborers could not be indentured (contracted to work for a specific number of years). This allowed owners to remove the opportunity for slaves to buy their freedom. Blacks in most southern states could not own property or sign contracts (such as a marriage contract). Slaves and their children were considered private property; helping a slave to escape was thievery.[10] In this context, George Bourne, a Presbyterian minister in Virginia and an anti-slavery pioneer, wrote in *The Book and Slavery Irreconcilable* (1816), "Reducing a *person* to a *thing*—a *man* to an *animal*. Such is 'a system of incurable injustice . . . the greatest practical evil that ever has inflicted the human race, and the severest and most extensive calamity recorded in the history of the world.' . . . Slavery with its abettors, is 'a mill-stone hanged about the neck' of the church, from which she must be loosened, or she will be 'drowned in the depth of the sea.'"[11] Partly because of his anti-slavery stand, Bourne was defrocked.[12]

About the same time, Albert Barnes, a Bible expositor, social reformer, and Presbyterian minister in Philadelphia, published *An Inquiry into the Scriptural Views of Slavery* (1857). In it, he explained how the scriptural teaching on slavery is not parallel to that regarding husband and wives, and parents and children: (1) servitude is "uniformly represented . . . as a *hard* condition"; (2) submission of slaves is spoken of as a *hard* condition, "one in which they were constantly liable to suffer wrong (1 Peter 2:18-19)"; (3) hence slaves were to cultivate the virtue of "*patience under wrong*"; and (4) Paul advised escape from servitude, if possible (see 1 Corinthians 7:21).[13]

1. Kenneth Barker, ed., *The NIV Study Bible* (Grand Rapids, MI: Zondervan, 1985), 1855.
2. J. D. Douglas, F. F. Bruce, J. I. Packer, N. Hillyer, D. Guthrie, A. R. Millard, and D. J. Wiseman, ed., *The New Bible Dictionary* (Carol Stream, IL: Tyndale, 1982), "Slave," 1198.
3. Francis Lyall, *Slaves, Citizens, Sons: Legal Metaphors in the Epistles* (Grand Rapids, MI: Zondervan, 1984), 35.
4. Lyall, 35.
5. Lyall, 36.
6. Lyall, 38.
7. Willard M. Swartley, *Slavery, Sabbath, War, and Women* (Scottdale, PA: Herald, 1983), 286, note 137.
8. Douglas, et. al., "Slave," 1198.
9. Lyall, 35.
10. Robert L. Cord, James A. Medeiros, and Walter S. Jones, *Political Science: An Introduction* (Englewood Cliffs, NJ: Prentice-Hall, 1974), 543.
11. Swartley, 53. From *The Book and Slavery Irreconcilable* (Philadelphia: J. M. Sanderson & Co., 1816), 111 and 109; quoted from William Pitt. Now available in *George Bourne and The Book and Slavery Irreconcilable* by John W. Christie and Dwight L. Dumond (Wilmington, DE: The Historical Society of Delaware and Philadelphia, The Presbyterian Historical Society, 1969), 103–196.
12. Swartley, 38.

13. Swartley, 52. From Albert Barnes, *An Inquiry into the Scriptural Views of Slavery* (New York: Negro Universities Press, 1969), 276–277; originally published by Parry & Macmillan in 1857. Barnes is the author of the well-known commentary *Barnes' Notes*, in which he also addresses the subject of slavery in comments on Isaiah 58:6 and Ephesians 6:5-9 (Swartley, 280).

PHILEMON 1-25

From Slave to Son

You might want to read the background before beginning your study of this letter.

Apphia . . . Archippus (verse 2). Probably Philemon's wife and their son.[1]

Onesimus (verse 10). The word means "useful" or "profitable." It was customary to give slaves names like this in the hope that, if they were called by such a name, their nature or conduct might come to match it.[2]

First impressions

Philemon is structured like Paul's other letters, with a greeting, the body of the letter, and a closing. This, however, is a very personal letter, in which Paul uses "I," rather than "we," as he had in his letter to the entire church at Colosse. Furthermore, he wrote this letter with his "own hand" (verse 19), rather than using a secretary, as he did for other letters.

Imagine the Colossian church gathered in Philemon's home, having just heard of the return of Tychicus and Onesimus (see Colossians 4:7-9). They are whispering among themselves, wondering what Philemon's response to the runaway slave—who is nowhere in sight—will be. Philemon gestures the group to silence and asks Tychicus to read Paul's letter to the church. They can't help eyeing Philemon when Tychicus gets to the part about slaves and their masters. What does it all mean? And where is Onesimus?

"I see discussion of Paul's letter is somewhat futile," chides Tychicus, as he watches the group squirm in anticipation, "until Philemon has read his own letter from Paul. Do you mind, brother?"

"Well, it's kind of personal," replies Philemon, "but allow me to read the parts that are important to the rest of the church here."

1. Read through Philemon several times. What is the letter about?

_____

_____

_____

_____

_____

2. What words or phrases can you find that express Paul's relationship with Philemon?

verse 1 _____

_____

verse 7 _____

_____

verse 17 _____

_____

verse 19 _____

_____

_____

verse 20 _____

_____

_____

verse 21 _____

_____

verse 22 _____

_____

Optional Application: How can you encourage someone with whom you have a personal relationship, using Paul's pattern from verses 4-7?

Greetings and prayers (verses 1-7)

After his greeting to the family and the rest of the church, Paul affirms his relationship with Philemon (see verses 4-7).

3. How does Paul encourage Philemon's spiritual growth?

verse 4 _____

_____

_____

_____

verse 6 _____

_____

_____

_____

4. What characteristics in Philemon does Paul affirm?

verse 5 _____

_____

_____

_____

verse 7 _____

_____

_____

_____

Optional Application: Write a letter to a friend that tells how he or she has given you joy and encouragement.

Study Skill — Chiasms
When a thought is structured like the Greek letter *chi (X)*, it is called a *chiasm*. Philemon 5 is an example of this literary device.[3] The NKJV translates it literally: "I hear of your love and of the faith which you have toward the Lord Jesus and toward all the saints." Here is how it looks as a chiasm:

love ╲   ╱ faith
      ╲   ╱
       ╲   ╱
        ╲   ╱
         ╲   ╱
          ╲   ╱
           ╳
the Lord Jesus   all the saints

The plea (verses 8-21)

5. a. How does Paul formulate his appeal for Onesimus (see verses 8-9)?

_____

_____

_____

_____

_____

  b. What does this tell you about Paul's view of his relationship with Philemon?

_____

_____

_____

_____

_____

6. What has happened to Onesimus since his arrival in Rome (see verse 10)?

_____

_____

128

_____

_____

_____

_____

7. How has Onesimus become worthy of his name (see verse 11)?

_____

_____

_____

_____

_____

8. What words or phrases does Paul use to express his relationship with Onesimus (see verses 10,12,16)?

_____

_____

_____

_____

_____

9. From our study of Colossians, we learned that in Christ there is neither slave nor free (see 3:11). Compare your list in question 8 with the list in question 2. How has Onesimus's relationship with his master changed?

_____

_____

_____

_____

For Thought and Discussion: Is there anyone whom you have the right to order, as Paul could order Philemon? Is there anyone who has the right to order you? Would you take orders from an apostle? A spiritual parent? A pastor? Why or why not?

129

10. How does Paul extend himself to persuade Philemon (see verses 17-19)?

_____

_____

_____

_____

11. a. What risks was Paul taking by allowing Philemon to make the final decisions regarding Onesimus?

_____

_____

_____

_____

b. How did Paul try to motivate Philemon to make a wise decision?

_____

_____

_____

_____

c. With these responses in mind, what can you learn from Paul about good leadership?

_____

_____

_____

_____

12. a. What risks do you think Onesimus was taking by returning to Philemon? How do you think he felt?

_____

_____

_____

_____

_____

b. Despite his feelings, Onesimus did what was right. Why do you think it was right for him to return?

_____

_____

_____

_____

_____

13. What lessons for Christians today, especially you, do you find in Philemon?

_____

_____

_____

_____

_____

14. How would you like to respond in prayer and/or action to what you have learned?

_____

_____

_____

_____

15. List any questions you have about this letter.

_____

_____

_____

_____

_____

One thing more (22-25)

As was often the case in ancient letters, a second matter to be discussed had to do with how and when the author planned to meet the recipient again. "Prepare a guest room for me," Paul says (verse 22). As a final affirmation of his relationship with Philemon and the church at Colosse, Paul expresses his desire to be with them again. We don't know how long it was before the "prisoner of Christ Jesus" (verse 9) was able to fulfill his desire.

For the group

Worship.

Read aloud.

Summarize. Ask someone to explain the situation that prompted the letter. Then ask someone else to summarize what Paul says.

Questions.

Group review. You might organize your final discussion around four questions: (1) What have you learned from your study of Colossians and Philemon? (2) How have you changed individually as a result of your study? (3) How has your life together changed as a result of your study? (4) Where will you go from here? You may be more able to see each other's growth than your own. Think about why change has or has not occurred. Try to encourage each other without expecting instant results.

Give everyone a chance to ask questions he or she still has about the letters to Colosse and to Philemon. See if you can answer them together, or if you need to assign research to someone.

Then, evaluate how well your group functioned during your study of Colossians and Philemon. (You might take a whole meeting for this.) Some questions you might ask are:

What did you learn about small-group study?
How well did the study help you grasp the letters to the Colossians and to Philemon?
What were the most important truths you discovered together about Christ?
What did you like best about your meetings?
What did you like least? What would you change?
How well did you meet the goals you set at your first meeting?
What are members' current needs? What will you do next?

1. F. F. Bruce, *The Epistles to the Colossians, to Philemon, and to the Ephesians* (Grand Rapids, MI: Eerdmans, 1984), 206.
2. Bruce, 213.
3. Kenneth Barker, ed., *The NIV Study Bible* (Grand Rapids, MI: Zondervan, 1985), 1856.

STUDY AIDS

For further information on the material covered in this study, consider the following sources. If your local bookstore does not have them, ask the bookstore to order them from the publishers, or you can look for them in a public university or seminary library. If they are out of print, you might be able to find them online.

Commentaries on Colossians and Philemon

Bruce, F. F. *The Epistles to the Colossians, to Philemon, and to the Ephesians,* New International Commentary on the New Testament (Eerdmans, 1984).
    Excellent on theology, word studies, and cross-references. Very good introduction to the setting in the Lycus Valley region of Asia Minor. Although Greek references and footnotes make it scholarly, a person can learn a great deal about Paul's message without knowledge of Greek.

Carson, Herbert M. *The Epistles of Paul to the Colossians and Philemon,* Tyndale New Testament Commentaries (Eerdmans, 1960).
    This little commentary is readable and brief. Excellent for the beginning student. Available in an inexpensive paperback edition.

Hendriksen, William. *The Epistles to the Colossians and Philemon,* New Testament Commentary (Baker, 1965).
    Very readable and inspiring, like good expository sermons on the text of Paul's letters. Hendriksen is concerned to show the relevance of the letters to modern Christians.

Lucas, R. C. *Fullness and Freedom: The Message of Colossians and Philemon,* The Bible Speaks Today Series (InterVarsity, 1980).

O'Brien, Peter T. *Colossians-Philemon,* Word Biblical Commentary (Nelson, 1982).
    Even more scholarly than Bruce and also longer, but with excellent commentary. The word studies are exceptional. You can skip over the Greek and still gain much.

Historical and background sources

Bruce, F. F. *New Testament History* (Doubleday, 1979).
A readable history of Herodian kings, Roman governors, philosophical schools, Jewish sects, Jesus, the early Jerusalem church, Paul, and early Gentile Christianity. Well-documented with footnotes for the serious student, but the notes do not intrude.

Bruce, F. F. *Paul, Apostle of the Heart Set Free* (Eerdmans, 1977).
Possibly the best book around on Paul's personality and ideas set in their historical context. Excellent both on Paul's teaching and his times. Very readable.

Cannon, George E. *The Use of Traditional Materials in Colossians: Their Significance for the Problems of Authenticity* (Mercer University, 1983).
Published as a doctoral dissertation, this is a fascinating history for the student interested in ancient origins of modern practices. A knowledge of Greek and Hebrew is encouraged but not required.

Harrison, E. F. *Introduction to the New Testament* (Eerdmans, 1971).
History from Alexander the Great—who made Greek culture dominant in the biblical world—through philosophies, pagan and Jewish religion, Jesus' ministry and teaching (the weakest section), and the spread of Christianity. Contains very good maps and photographs of the land, art, and architecture of New Testament times.

Packer, James I., Merrill C. Tenney, William White, Jr. *The Bible Almanac* (Thomas Nelson, 1980).
One of the most accessible handbooks of the people of the Bible and how they lived. Lots of photos and illustrations liven an already readable text.

Oesterley, W. O. E. *The Jewish Background of the Christian Liturgy* (Peter Smith, 1965).
Much more readable than Cannon (the Hebrew is transliterated) and focusing on Jewish backgrounds. Very interesting reading, particularly if you love the language of worship.

Histories, concordances, dictionaries, and handbooks

A **concordance** lists words of the Bible alphabetically along with each verse in which the word appears. It lets you do your own word studies. An *exhaustive* concordance lists every word used in a given translation, while an *abridged* or *complete* concordance omits either some words, some occurrences of the word, or both.

Two of the three best exhaustive concordances are the venerable *Strong's Exhaustive Concordance* and *Young's Analytical Concordance to the Bible.* Both are available based on the King James Version and the New American Standard Bible. *Strong's* has an index in which you can find out which Greek or Hebrew word is used in a given English verse (although its information is occasionally outdated). *Young's* breaks up each English word it translates. Neither concordance requires knowledge of the original languages.

Perhaps the best exhaustive concordance currently on the market is *The NIV Exhaustive Concordance.* It features a Hebrew-to-English and a Greek-to-English lexicon (based on the eclectic text underlying the NIV), which are also keyed to *Strong's* numbering system.

Among other good, less expensive concordances, *Cruden's Complete Concordance* is keyed to the King James and Revised Versions, the *NIV Complete Concordance* is keyed to the New International Version. These include all references to every word included, but they omit "minor" words. They also lack indexes to the original languages.

A **Bible dictionary** or **Bible encyclopedia** alphabetically lists articles about people, places, doctrines, important words, customs, and geography of the Bible.

The New Bible Dictionary, edited by J. D. Douglas, F. F. Bruce, J. I. Packer, N. Hillyer, D. Guthrie, A. R. Millard, and D. J. Wiseman (Tyndale, 1982) is more comprehensive than most dictionaries. Its 1,300 pages include quantities of information along with excellent maps, charts, diagrams, and an index for cross-referencing.

Unger's Bible Dictionary by Merrill F. Unger (Moody, 1979) is equally good and is available in an inexpensive paperback edition.

The Zondervan Pictorial Encyclopedia edited by Merrill C. Tenney (Zondervan, 1975, 1976) is excellent and exhaustive, and has been revised and updated. Its five 1,000-page volumes represent a significant financial investment, however, and all but very serious students may prefer to use it at a church, public college, or seminary library.

Unlike a Bible dictionary in the above sense, *Vine's Expository Dictionary of New Testament Words* by W. E. Vine (various publishers) alphabetically lists major words used in the *King James Version* and defines each New Testament Greek word that the KJV translates with its English word. Vine's also lists verse references where that Greek word appears, so you can do your own cross-references and word studies without knowing any Greek.

Vine's is a good, basic book for beginners, but it is much less complete than other Greek helps for English speakers. More serious students might prefer *The New International Dictionary of New Testament Theology*, edited by Colin Brown (Zondervan) or *The Theological Dictionary of the New Testament* by Gerhard Kittel and Gerhard Friedrich, abridged in one volume by Geoffrey W. Bromiley (Eerdmans).

Bible atlases and map books

A **Bible atlas** can be a great aid to understanding what is going on in a book of the Bible and how geography affected events. Here are a few good choices:

The Macmillan Atlas by Yohanan Aharoni and Michael Avi-Yonah (Macmillan, 1968, 1977) contains 264 maps, 89 photos, and 12 graphics. The many maps of individual events portray battles, movements of people, and changes of boundaries in detail.

The New Bible Atlas by J. J. Bimson and J. P. Kane (Tyndale, 1985) has 73 maps, 34 photos, and 34 graphics. Its evangelical perspective, concise and helpful text, and excellent research make it a very good choice, but its greatest strength lies in outstanding graphics, such as cross-sections of the Dead Sea.

The Bible Mapbook by Simon Jenkins (Lion, 1984) is much shorter and less expensive than most other atlases, so it offers a good first taste of the usefulness of maps. It contains 91 simple maps, very little text, and 20 graphics. Some of the graphics are computer-generated and intriguing.

The Moody Atlas of Bible Lands by Barry J. Beitzel (Moody, 1984) is scholarly, evangelical, and full of theological text, indexes, and references. This admirable reference work will be too deep and costly for some, but Beitzel shows vividly how God prepared the land of Israel perfectly for the acts of salvation He planned to accomplish in it.

A **handbook** of biblical customs can also be useful. Some good ones are *Today's Handbook of Bible Times and Customs* by William L. Coleman (Bethany, 1984) and the less detailed *Daily Life in Bible Times* (Nelson, 1982).

For small-group leaders

Barker, Steve et al. *The Small Group Leader's Handbook* (Intervarsity, 1982). Written by an InterVarsity small group with college students primarily in mind. It includes information on small-group dynamics and how to lead in light of them, and many ideas for worship, building community, and outreach. It has a good chapter on doing inductive Bible study.

Griffin, Em. *Getting Together: A Guide for Good Groups* (Intervarsity, 1982). Applies to all kinds of groups, not just Bible studies. From his own experience, Griffin draws deep insights into why people join groups; how people relate to each other; and principles of leadership, decision making, and discussions. It is fun to read, but its 229 pages will take more time than the above book.

Hunt, Gladys. *You Can Start a Bible Study Group* (Harold Shaw, 1984). Builds on Hunt's thirty years of experience leading groups. This book is wonderfully focused on God's enabling. It is both clear and applicable for Bible study groups of all kinds.

McBride, Neal F. *How to Build a Small Groups Ministry* (NavPress, 1994).

This hands-on workbook for pastors and lay leaders includes everything you need to know to develop a plan that fits your unique church. Through basic principles, case studies, and worksheets, McBride leads you through twelve logical steps for organizing and administering a small groups ministry.

McBride, Neal F. *How to Lead Small Groups* (NavPress, 1990).
Covers leadership skills for all kinds of small groups—Bible study, fellowship, task, and support groups. Filled with step-by-step guidance and practical exercises to help you grasp the critical aspects of small group leadership and dynamics.

Bible study methods

Braga, James. *How to Study the Bible* (Multnomah, 1982).
Clear chapters on a variety of approaches to Bible study: synthetic, geographical, cultural, historical, doctrinal, practical, and so on. Designed to help the ordinary person without seminary training to use these approaches.

Fee, Gordon, and Douglas Stuart. *How to Read the Bible for All Its Worth* (Zondervan, 1982).
After explaining in general what interpretation and application are, Fee and Stuart offer chapters on interpreting and applying the different kinds of writing in the Bible: Epistles, Gospels, Old Testament Law, Old Testament narrative, the Prophets, Psalms, Wisdom, and Revelation. Fee and Stuart also suggest good commentaries on each biblical book. They write as evangelical scholars who personally recognize Scripture as God's Word for their daily lives.

Jensen, Irving L. *Independent Bible Study* (Moody, 1963) and *Enjoy Your Bible* (Moody, 1962).
The former is a comprehensive introduction to the inductive Bible study method, especially the use of synthetic charts. The latter is a simpler introduction to the subject.

Wald, Oletta. *The Joy of Discovery in Bible Study* (Augsburg, 1975).
Wald focuses on issues such as how to observe all that is in a text, how to ask questions of a text, how to use grammar and passage structure to see the writer's point, and so on. Very helpful on these subjects.

Encounter God's Word
Experience LifeChange

LifeChange by The Navigators

The LifeChange Bible study series can help you grow in Christ-likeness through a life-changing encounter with God's Word. Discover what the Bible says, and develop the skills and desire to dig even deeper into God's Word. Each study includes study aids and discussion questions.

NAVESSENTIALS

Voices of The Navigators—Past, Present, and Future

NavEssentials offer core Navigator messages from such authors as Jim Downing, LeRoy Eims, Mike Treneer, and more — at an affordable price. This new series will deeply influence generations in the movement of discipleship. Learn from the old and new messages of The Navigators how powerful and transformational the life of a disciple truly is.

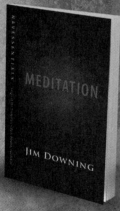  

Meditation
by Jim Downing
9781615217250

Advancing the Gospel
by Mike Treneer
9781617471575

The Triumph of Surrender
by William M. Fletcher
9781615219070

Available wherever books are sold. NAVPRESS